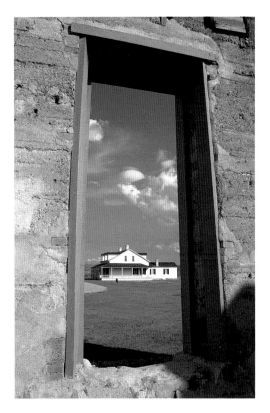

Wyoming's
HISTORIC FORTS

by Barbara Fifer

Photography by Fred Pflughoft and David M. Morris

FARCOUNTRY
PRESS

Front cover: Enlisted men's barracks at Fort Laramie National Historic Site. DAVID M. MORRIS
Back cover: Ice house at Fort Bridger National Historic Site. FRED PFLUGHOFT
Front flap photos: Reenactors bring the past to the present. FRED PFLUGHOFT
Title page: Fort Laramie National Historic Site. FRED PFLUGHOFT

ISBN 1-56037-191-9

Photographs © by the photographers as credited
© 2002 Farcountry Press

Created, produced, and designed in the United States. Printed in Korea.

✑ ─ CONTENTS ─ ✑

Wyoming's Historic Forts

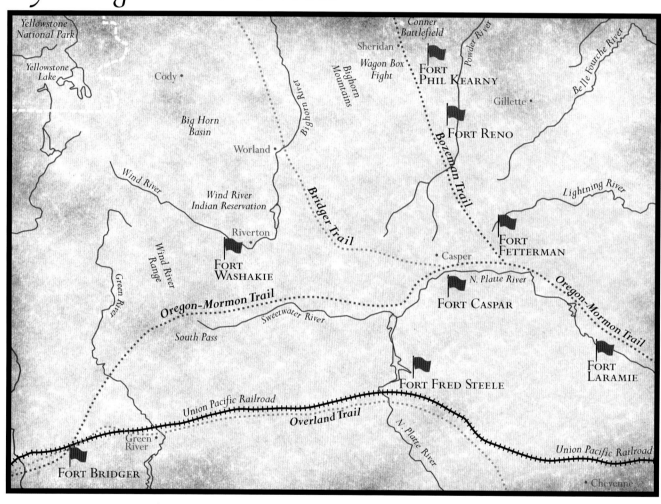

Yellowstone National Park
Yellowstone Lake
Cody
Big Horn Basin
Worland
Wind River
Wind River Indian Reservation
Riverton
FORT WASHAKIE
Green River
Wind River Range
South Pass
Oregon-Mormon Trail
Sweetwater River
Bighorn River
Bighorn Mountains
Wagon Box Fight
Conner Battlefield
Sheridan
FORT PHIL KEARNY
Powder River
Gillette
Belle Fourche River
Bridger Trail
Bozeman Trail
FORT RENO
Lightning River
FORT FETTERMAN
Casper
N. Platte River
FORT CASPAR
Oregon-Mormon Trail
FORT LARAMIE
FORT FRED STEELE
Union Pacific Railroad
Overland Trail
N. Platte River
Green River
FORT BRIDGER
Union Pacific Railroad
Cheyenne

INTRODUCTION

Wyoming's historic forts offer a colorful panorama of stories of Native Americans, mountain men, traders, wagon train emigrants, frontier soldiers, railroad builders—up to intrepid early-day "autoists." Some forts today offer surviving or reconstructed buildings, with exhibits, programs, and costumed interpreters who recall other eras, surrounding visitors with sights, sounds, and smells now exotic but once commonplace. Other forts live only in memory, their sites marked by interpretive signs that lead our imaginations to see the long-gone buildings and people. One fort even still serves its original purpose.

In this book, text and illustrations are arranged in rough chronological order, and reading all the way through it gives a partial history of Wyoming. Individual forts may have more to do with certain eras than others, while some saw many generations of changes.

Although the word "fort" may conjure military images, not every fort began or ended that way. Some were trading posts that later served wagon trains, stagecoaches, or Pony Express riders. Some were purely military, but their very presence invited surrounding civilian settlements.

This book doesn't cover every military site or trading post that once carried the name "fort." Rather, we tell the stories and preserve the images of forts that Wyoming people have chosen to protect, places worth visiting now to learn more about how people of the past shaped Wyoming and the United States.

The Fort Laramie officers' quarters, at left, were built in 1881 to replace an adobe structure that had stood since 1855. The restored bachelor officers' barracks, at right, was built as soon as the army took over the fort in 1849. FRED PFLUGHOFT

FORT LARAMIE

EST. 1834

The 1832 fur trade rendezvous in Pierre's Hole, in what is now Wyoming, had just ended. In the July heat, some friendly Flathead Indians were traveling away from the trading meet with American trappers when they ran into 200 Gros Ventre (Atsina) Indians. A Gros Ventre leader walked forward carrying a truce flag, but one of the Flatheads—his traditional enemies—killed him. The fight that followed left ten Gros Ventre dead, but they had killed five mountain men and seven Flatheads.

Mountain man William Sublette was wounded during the battle, but fellow fur trader Robert Campbell saved him from death. The two entered into a business partnership that same year. At age thirty-three, Sublette had a decade of experience under his belt, and Campbell, an Irish immigrant who was five years younger, had seven years.

The pair set up their "Fort William" near Fort Union, a post run by John Jacob Astor's powerful American Fur Company's where the Yellowstone River ran into the Missouri (then at today's Montana–North Dakota border; the river's mouth has since migrated a few miles east). Historians think that, rather than expecting to compete, Sublette hoped to goad the giant into dealing with his partner and him. Whatever their motive, the upstarts were driven out within two years.

Moving south to Laramai's Point near where the Laramie River flows into the North Platte, Campbell and Sublette built their second Fort William.

That same year of 1834, Astor sold his interests in the American Fur Company that he'd founded twenty-six years before. Believing that the beaver trade was beginning to decline, he was more farsighted than many

Artist Alfred Jacob Miller, traveling with the sport-hunting party of Sir William Drummond Stewart, painted the summer trading encampment at Fort William in 1837. WYOMING STATE ARCHIVES

of his competitors. In the next few years, smaller fur companies were gobbled up one by one by the Astor-less company that still was called the American Fur Company, but officially was Pratte-Chouteau & Company.

The firm of Sublette and Campbell sold Fort William II to Fontenelle, Fitzpatrick & Company in 1835, which in turn sold it to American Fur the next year. The two mountain men settled with their families in St. Louis, Missouri, continuing in trade and politics for the rest of their lives (Sublette died in 1845, Campbell surviving him by more than three decades). But they had started the first permanent settlement in the future state of Wyoming.

Under the American Fur Company, the isolated fort was a great success—until Fort Platte was built a mile away between 1839 and 1840. Spurred by the competition, American Fur dismantled log Fort William, and put up

This 1842 sketch of Fort John (as viewed from across the Laramie River) shows the brand-new fort that the American Fur Company built to replace Sublette and Campbell's Fort William. It was on the river bank behind where the captain's quarters now stands. KANSAS STATE HISTORICAL SOCIETY

a larger adobe-and-wood complex that they christened "Fort John." But, trappers, traders, and other local people continued to call the bigger fort "Laramie."

Soon a new kind of white person began to travel the old fur trail through the area. One small party of wagon-train emigrants stopped at Fort Laramie in 1841, and a thousand emigrants in 1843, but the peak year wasn't until 1852, when fifty times that many passed by. These wagon trains were heading for South Pass on the Oregon Trail, and onward to claim land in the Oregon Country

The earliest known photograph of the military post Fort Laramie dates from 1858, and shows the remains of Fort John (at left) and the bachelor officers' quarters, center. WYOMING STATE ARCHIVES

or, beginning in 1849, to rush to California for gold. After they rested and prepared at Fort Laramie, their wagons began to climb into the mountains.

From 1834 on, thousands of Sioux, Cheyenne, and Arapaho people had come to Fort Laramie to trade, and some decided to live nearby. At first, trading was comfortable and friendly, but some Sioux bands became anxious as they saw more and more whites passing through this land. The whites' animals ate the grass, dirtied the water sources, and made a lot of noise. All that drove away buffalo herds that the Plains Indians depended on for food, clothing, and tools and other implements. Sometimes young Lakota Sioux men approached the trains trying to collect tolls of coffee and tobacco to offset their losses (which whites misinterpreted as "begging"), but they almost never attacked the strangers.

In 1851, Indian agent (and one of the men who had bought Fort William from Sublette and Campbell) Thomas Fitzpatrick negotiated a treaty at Fort Laramie. Sioux,

Cheyenne, Gros Ventre, Crow, Arikara, Assiniboine, Arapaho, and Mandan Indians agreed not to threaten wagon trains, in return for receiving fifty years of annual supply shipments—which term the U.S. Senate shortened to fifteen years. But, misunderstanding that the Indian nations were not organized like the United States government, Superintendent of Indian Affairs D.D. Mitchell insisted that leaders who signed did so for all their people. Indian people who hadn't signed and didn't agree with the treaty, however, simply ignored it.

Fort Laramie was the site of several major treaty negotiations over the years. Here negotiators meet in 1868 over Red Cloud's War. AMERICAN HERITAGE CENTER, UNIVERSITY OF WYOMING

By the late 1840s, Fort Laramie did more business selling supplies to emigrant trains than in reselling furs. Citizens were calling for more military troops to protect overland wagon trains, and in 1849 the army purchased Fort Laramie. By the time of Fitzpatrick's treaty, Laramie had become a military fort.

The first soldiers assigned here were put to work building some of the structures needed, and eventually their own and their officers' quarters, stables, and the all-important

bakery ringed the large parade ground. The adobe Fort John was left to decay until being torn down in 1862. Eight years later, the Captain's Quarters arose behind its old location.

The fort's soldiers fought their first Indian battle in 1854, when an inexperienced second lieutenant, John L. Grattan, tried to handle a minor incident. Thousands of Sioux were camped near Fort Laramie—and the Overland Trail—awaiting that year's annuities. When a cow wandered off from a Mormon wagon train and into their camp, a Sioux man killed it. A chief in the camp imme-

diately offered generous repayment in horses, but the train's wagon master insisted on punishment. Fort Laramie's commander sent Grattan to arrest the culprit.

Said to have been boasting how he could show Native Americans who was boss, Grattan borrowed a trader's interpreter and took him, along with twenty-nine soldiers, and not one—but two—cannons, into the Sioux camp. The drunk interpreter, combined with Grattan's threats and the soldiers' raised guns, caused a battle. No one knows who fired the first shot, but all the army men were killed (along with Conquering Bear, who had

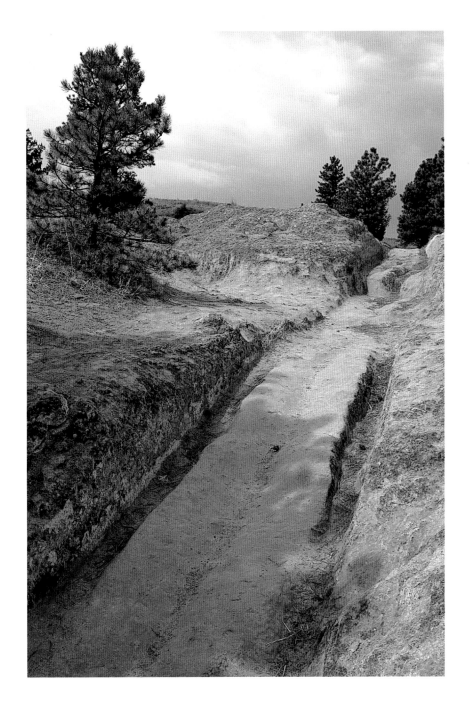

Thousands and thousands of heavily loaded Conestoga and freight wagons traveling the Oregon Trail in all kinds of weather left deep ruts that made driving difficult. At places, such as here at the town of Guernsey near Fort Laramie, the actual trail is still visible.
FRED PFLUGHOFT

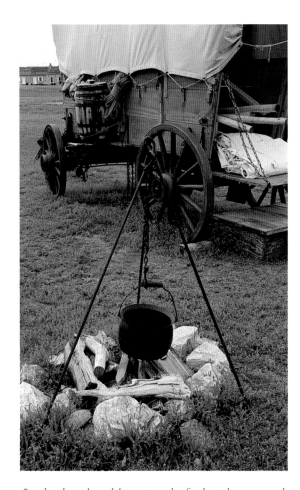

Bread, salt pork, and beans—staples for long-distance travel such as by wagon train—had to be cooked over or in open fires fueled by whatever was available: wood if you were lucky, or brush, or buffalo chips. FRED PFLUGHOFT

offered those horses), and the annuity store-houses raided and emptied, before the Sioux left the area. Cooler heads among older Sioux leaders were all that kept the warriors from destroying the fort that day. One young boy in the crowd, who took in the whole event, would become the great war leader Crazy Horse.

An army expedition sent out the next year, 1855, to punish the Sioux fed a simmering fire that would burn into the 1870s, and shape the stories of other historic Wyoming forts.

Then, in 1865, Fort Laramie commander Colonel Thomas Moonlight made a disastrous decision that fed Plains Indian rage for years to come. Two Sioux chiefs, Two Face and Black Foot, had come upon a white woman and her baby who were captives of their allies, the Cheyenne. Well intentioned, the chiefs bought the mother and child's freedom and took them to Fort Laramie to return to their people. Moonlight, against the protests of other officers, hanged the two leaders—the most humiliating death for a Plains warrior—and even kept their bodies on display for months.

The longer-term effects of these two

Soldiers drill on the west end of the parade ground in the 1880s, with the commander's quarters at left. WYOMING STATE ARCHIVES

The Lieutenant Colonel's Quarters today is called the Burt House after Lt. Col. Andrew Burt and his wife, Elizabeth, who lived here in 1887-1888. FRED PFLUGHOFT

events played out far from Fort Laramie, as Sioux and Cheyenne warriors sought revenge in battles small and large fought in Wyoming and Montana, ending with their victory over the Seventh Cavalry at the Little Bighorn in 1876. For the most part, soldiers here rode as escorts for wagon trains and, later, stagecoaches and telegraph builders. The army never even built a palisade fence— or any other kind—and so Fort Laramie (like most western posts) looked more like a village than a fortification.

Its location on the central transcontinental trail made the fort a natural Pony Express stop, "the Pony" as people called it lasted only a year and a half until the transcontinental telegraph—also with a station at Fort Laramie—replaced it.

In the Post Surgeon's Quarters, the parlor is furnished to reflect the doctor's high social position, showing stylish furniture and decorations of 1880, when the original building was five years old. Despite such relative amenities on the frontier, the average stay of a Fort Laramie post surgeon was only eight months. DAVID M. MORRIS

In the 1860s, Fort Laramie became a stop on Ben Holliday's Overland Stage Line, and then that of Wells, Fargo and Company, which absorbed the Overland. In "only" twenty-one days of bumpy, filthy, and totally uncomfortable round-the-clock travel, pas- sengers could reach California from St. Louis. Their sole respites were stage stops about ten to fifteen miles apart—for the horses' bene- fit—and stops for often-terrible, always expensive, meals. If a passenger stopped to sleep at the occasional "home" station that

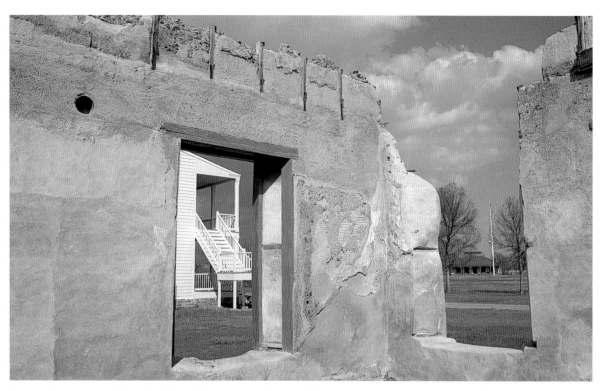

Looking through ruins of the 1881 Officers' Quarters to the Bachelor Officers' Quarters, the oldest standing building in Wyoming.
FRED PFLUGHOFT

offered primitive lodging, he was gambling on whether the next crowded coach would have a seat to offer.

During the last two decades of its military service—the 1870s and 1880s—Fort Laramie was a post where soldiers drilled and waited to be called to action elsewhere. In May of 1876, all but twenty-nine of them were sent to join the three-pronged pincer movement against the Sioux and Cheyenne, assigned to General George Crook and fight-ing in the Battle of the Rosebud in Montana Territory. (See Fort Fetterman chapter.) Another arm of the pincer included Colonel George Custer's Seventh Cavalry, which found the Indians' mass encampment on the Little Bighorn River.

Over the years, buildings were erected continuously at Fort Laramie, both replace-ments for old ones and structures added as need arose. By the time the army closed the fort in 1890, sixty buildings stood here. They

Left: In 1939, a year after being named a national monument, Fort Laramie had few of its sixty buildings left, and those survivors were in sad shape. WYOMING STATE ARCHIVES

Below: Travel by Overland Stage was uncomfortable and expensive, and it took twenty-one days to reach California from St. Louis. But, in the 1860s, the only alternative was spending months on an ocean-going ship. WYOMING STATE ARCHIVES

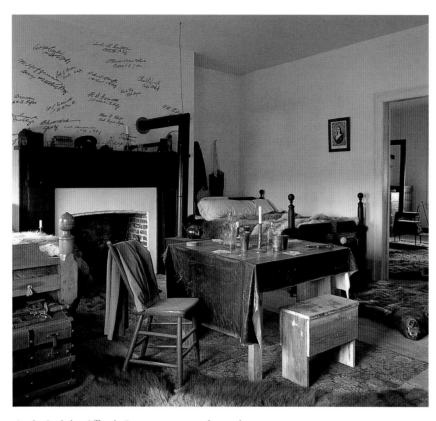

In the Bachelor Officer's Quarters, visitors today see how some single officers at frontier posts of the mid-1850s spent their winter evenings. The furniture shows that they used some manufactured pieces, and built their own as needed. Nineteen-century accounts refer to the structure as "Bedlam," the nickname of the Hospital of St. Mary of Bethlehem in London, England, an ancient insane asylum. DAVID M. MORRIS

were sold off to homesteaders, who recycled many buildings for farm use.

Those buildings that remained were left to wind and weather until 1937, when the State of Wyoming placed the site in trust and gave it to the federal government. President Franklin D. Roosevelt proclaimed Fort Laramie National Monument the following year.

Today, Fort Laramie National Historic Site's restored and preserved buildings are maintained by the National Park Service. During the summer, costumed interpreters help bring the fort to life as it was in its rich and diverse past, when Fort Laramie was the "crossroads of the west."

A hand-made quilt decorates the ornate double bed for the captain and his lady, with a cradle handy for their youngest child, in the master bedroom of the Captain's Quarters. *DAVID M. MORRIS*

The kitchen in the Captain's Quarters would have been the bailiwick of a hired cook, possibly the wife of an enlisted man. She had to work all day long to prepare meals on the wood burning stove, keep hot water available in the boiler, and wash dishes. *DAVID M. MORRIS*

Above: Originally built in 1870, the Captain's Quarters was a duplex. FRED PFLUGHOFT

Right: Personal treasures, carefully packed to carry from assignment to assignment, combine with Western artifacts like arrows and a mountain goat head in the parlor of the Captain's Quarters, where guests were received and could be entertained with evening "musicales" during the long winters. DAVID M. MORRIS

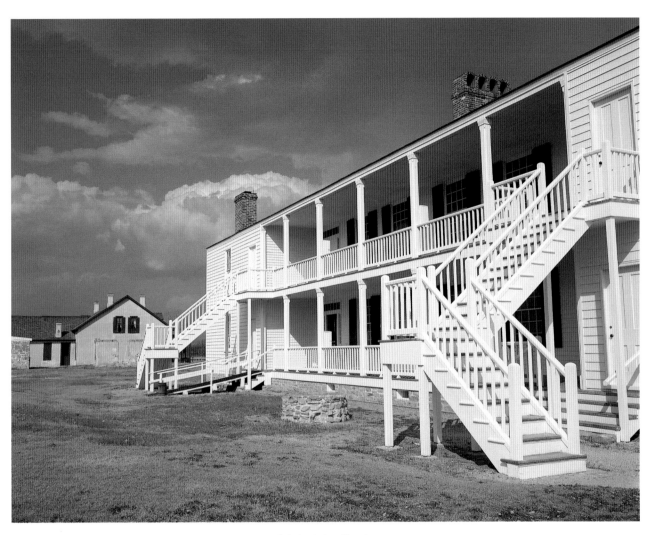

On Christmas Night, 1866, Portugee Phillips ran up the steps of the bachelor officers' quarters to interrupt a party with the news of the Fetterman battle and the endangered survivors at Fort Phil Kearny. FRED PFLUGHOFT

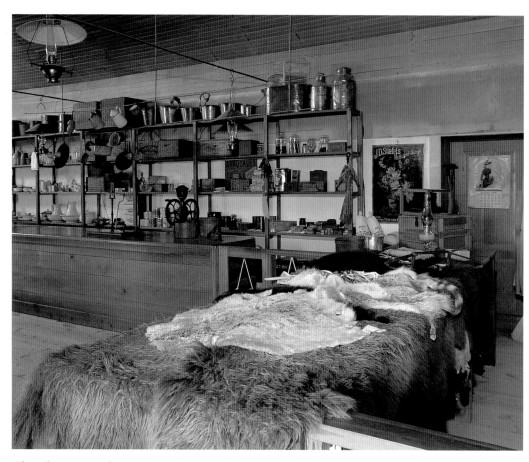

The sutler, or post trader, was a civilian who obtained a contract from the government to operate his store inside the fort. He traded with anyone he wanted to, so bought furs from Indians and mountain men, and sold supplies to emigrant wagon trains—as well as stocking what soldiers and their families might want beyond army-issued rations. Note the trade beads with the furs on the counter: different Indian nations preferred different colors, so the sutler would have kept the colors that local tribes wanted. He would offer a certain number of feet of strung beads for a given pelt. The building dates from 1849, but today is fitted out as in 1876. DAVID M. MORRIS

Right: The Old Guardhouse, built in 1866, saw soldiers who'd gotten into trouble sleeping on the floor without bedding, and with no heat or interior light. FRED PFLUGHOFT

Below: When this New Guardhouse opened as the fort's jail in 1876, it had the great improvements of better ventilation and straw mattresses (but no beds to put them on). FRED PFLUGHOFT

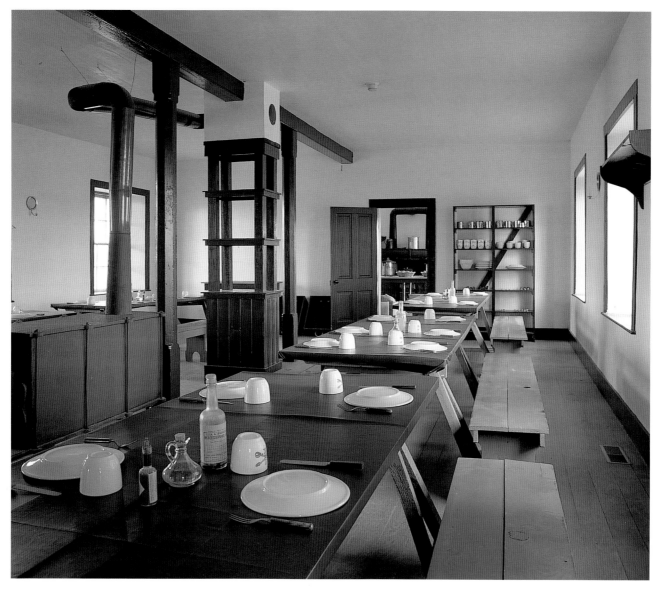

Simple condiments in the Enlisted Men's Mess could be used to cover up the "slightly off" taste of meat that was spoiling. DAVID M. MORRIS

When you're mixing and kneading enough bread dough for 300 or more pound-and-a-half loaves a day, spoons and mixing bowls aren't enough, as seen by the practical trough setup in the Old Bakery. *DAVID M. MORRIS*

The Pony Express

*I*ts story is dramatic, its life was short, and it helped bankrupt a company, but the Pony Express remains a powerful image of courage on the Western frontier.

Picture the lone rider galloping from station to station, no matter what the weather or how rough the land, determined to let nothing slow or stop the mail. Better yet, let Mark Twain describe what he saw in 1861, as he rode west on a stagecoach:

FRED PFLUGHOFT

"The passengers eagerly await the spectacle of an encounter with a Pony Express rider racing his load of mail to its next transfer point.

"Presently the driver exclaims:"'Here he comes!'

"Every neck is stretched further, and every eye strained wider. Away across the endless dead level of the prairie a black speck appears against the sky, and it is plain that it moves. Well, I should think so! In a second or two it becomes a horse and rider rising and falling, rising and falling—sweeping toward us nearer and nearer and still nearer—growing more and more distinct, more and more sharply defined—nearer and still nearer, and the flutter of the hoofs comes faintly to the ear—another instant a whoop and a hurrah from our upper deck, a wave of the rider's hand, but no reply, and a man and horse burst past our excited faces, and go winging away like a belated fragment of a storm!"

From Sacramento, California, to St. Joseph, Missouri, Pony Express remount stations were usually ten to fifteen miles apart. During his normal shift, a rider changed horses at three to four or more stations—as fast as he possibly could leap from the tired horse, lifting the mail and slinging it onto the saddle of the fresh horse the station attendant held ready. The rider was required to be on his way before two minutes had passed.

For security as well as the quick change of horses, the mail was carried in a "mochila," a rectangular leather skirt with holes for the saddles's horn and cantle, on which the rider sat. At each corner was a padlocked hard-leather box to hold letters written on the thinnest of tissue.

As they had to be—it cost a little over one hundred of today's dollars to mail a half-ounce letter.

Riders (many in their teens, and all of them male) could not weigh more than 120 pounds, but the horses stood as tall as fifteen hands high. A modern horse owner describes the relative size of man and beast as that of a jockey mounted on a thoroughbred. The custom-made saddles weighed one third what regular saddles did, and the entire kit—saddle, mochila, and bridle— totalled only thirteen pounds. A horse ran only from one station to the next, where stock tenders waited to care for it. About eighty riders (a complete company listing has never been found) worked for the Pony Express, but 400 men were employed as stock tenders, station keepers, and route superintendents.

William Henry Jackson portrayed a Pony Express riding awaiting placement of the mochila before springing onto his horse and taking off. WYOMING STATE ARCHIVES

When Russell, Majors and Waddell sent their first Pony Express riders out on April 3, 1860, they hoped the extremely fast service would win them the government mail contract then held by the Overland Mail Company. By sending their riders across the "central route"—through Wyoming—they could deliver sooner than the Overland, whose stagecoaches went across Texas to California. Arriving at Sacramento, the Pony Express rider generally boarded a coastal steamer to reach San Francisco.

On that initial trip, when an eastbound rider met one headed west, they passed each other just east of the Great Salt Lake. The few letters one carried moved from Missouri to the West Coast in only eight days, compared to at least three weeks by stagecoach, and months by ship, train, and ship to go via Panama.

A year later, Pony Express riders carried news westward that the Union had split and the nation was fighting a civil war. Communication between gold-rich California and the Union became even more important, and both telegraph and railroad lines were being built as quickly as possible across the continent—following the central route Russell, Majors and Waddell touted.

Some Indian nations along the Pony Express route thought that attacking the remount stations and the riders would stop these unwelcome whites from encroaching on their land. They killed at least three riders and two station personnel, and burned more than one station.

On the route not far west of Fort Laramie in 1860, fourteen-year-old (and youngest Pony Express rider) William F. Cody made the service's longest nonstop ride. Finishing his own ride from Red Buttes (near today's Casper) to Three Crossings, the future "Buffalo Bill" learned that the relief rider had been killed, and so he pushed on another seventy-six miles to Rocky Ridge station. Handing off the mailbag to the rider waiting there, Cody immediately headed back to Red Buttes. He rode for twenty-one hours and forty minutes, and used twenty-one horses in covering 322 miles.

The year before, twenty-year-old "Pony Bob" Haslam had set the record for longest Pony Express round-trip, but he had a nine-hour rest in the middle of his 380-mile race east then back west in Nevada.

The fastest Pony Express trip of all is recorded as taking seven days and seventeen hours, but the company had hired extra men and placed fresh horses every ten miles in order to speed delivering the transcription of President Lincoln's inaugural address from St. Joseph (where it was received by telegraph) to Sacramento.

As soon as the telegraph line was completed to the West Coast, there was no more need for the Pony Express, and it ended in late October 1861. The money the company spent on it, along with other financial factors, bankrupted the creators. To deliver fewer than 35,000 letters, Russell, Majors and Waddell lost at least $2 million in today's dollars, along with the lives of several employees.

But the myth remains, and people still pause along the Pony Express route across Wyoming, just in case "the flutter of the hoofs comes faintly to the ear..."

This steel engraving portrays a Pony Express rider in 1861 saluting builders of the telegraph line that would soon put him out of work. WYOMING STATE ARCHIVES

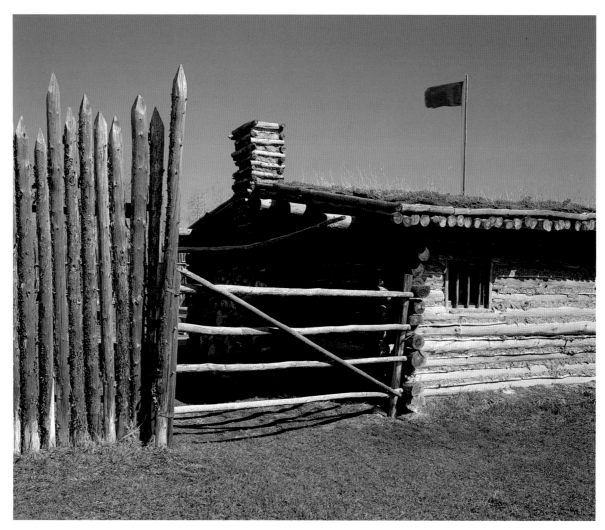

At Fort Bridger State Historic Site stands this replica of Bridger and Vasquez's original trading post. FRED PFLUGHOFT

FORT BRIDGER

EST. 1843

Fort Bridger saw an intriguing mixture of people pass through its gates as the Wyoming frontier changed. Mountain men trading with Indians, Mormon emigrants riding in wagons or pushing handcarts, homesteaders and California gold rushers in their wagon trains, and raunchy railroad-building crews—all passed by here on the fur-trading path that developed into the Oregon Trail. Fort Bridger began life as a trading post and ended up a military garrison.

Its namesake was the "been there done that" man of the American West in the 19th

Long after his eleven years at Fort Bridger, "Old Gabe," as mountain men called him— Jim Bridger himself—sat for the camera, which seemed to catch a faraway look in his failing eyes. MONTANA HISTORICAL SOCIETY

century. Jim Bridger had been born in 1804 in Virginia but raised on what was then the frontier near St. Louis, Missouri. As a mountain man and fur trader for twenty-one years, he traveled from Montana to New Mexico, St. Louis to the Great Salt Lake. Wounded in an Indian battle when he was twenty-eight, Bridger had part of an arrow in his back for three years, until he ran into Dr. Marcus Whitman, who was out west looking for a site to build a mission. During Bridger's decade at Fort Bridger, he guided surveying parties in the Rocky Mountains and, after

leaving the fort, guided military and civilian expeditions—among them, the first official explorers to see future Yellowstone National Park.

Bridger married three times, each time to an Indian woman, was widowed twice, and fathered six children he sent to mission schools. Only failing eyesight could drive him back to "civilization," which it did when he was in his early sixties. With his third wife, Mary, and the children, the man nicknamed

"Old Gabe" settled in Westport, Missouri—then equal to Independence and St. Joseph as an outfitting center for the westward bound. There he stayed for the last fifteen years of his life, dispensing advice and tall tales.

Louis Vasquez was six years older than his lifelong friend and partner in Fort Bridger. He had worked in all kinds of frontier trading: as a mountain man, supplying the annual rendezvous, trading with various Indian tribes, hauling supplies up the Sante Fe Trail to northern trading posts, and partnering with Andrew Sublette to create the successful Fort Vasquez north of today's Denver. Vasquez once wrote his brother that his goal was "to make money or die," and he worked hard to reach it.

Just as the fur trade was beginning to slow down in 1842 and overland wagon trains to increase, Bridger and Vasquez saw there was money in supplying the emigrants. They selected this beautiful valley on the Blacks Fork of the Green River along a trail that fur traders had been using for years. The view to the south was the Uinta Mountains, and the valley's many streams supported trees and shrubs along their courses.

More importantly, the location was a lit-

In the Bridger and Vasquez post reconstruction, this replica blacksmith shop includes hand-pumped bellows to heat the fire in the stone forge, an anvil for shaping hot metal, and a wooden water bucket for cooling the new item. DAVID M. MORRIS

Free Trappers & Rendezvous

*T*he word went out among mountain men in the summer of 1825, something like a party invitation: Come to the rendezvous on Henrys Fork of the Green River in Wyoming. There'll be plenty of food, singing and dancing, contests like ax-throwing, knife-throwing, and arm-wrestling, and news and store-bought goods from back in the States. Visit with your old friends and make some new ones!

Jim Bridger went, and he'd miss only a few of these uproarious trading socials that were held up through the summer of 1840.

Before—and after—those years, mountain men went to trading posts to sell the furs they had trapped or bought from Indians. In return, they got supplies for their next year in the northern Rocky Mountains. Then William Henry Ashley adopted the rendezvous idea from Scottish trader Donald McKenzie, who held Snake River rendezvous west of the Rockies from 1816 to 1832.

Ashley and his traders loaded pack trains with what mountain men had nowhere else to buy, things they could use themselves or as gifts or trade items for Indians. This meant manufactured items like gunpowder and lead; guns, hatchets, knives and other tools; cast-iron Dutch ovens and frying pans; and blankets and lengths of cloth. The "free trappers"—men under contract to no single fur company—worked far from settlements that had stores, living alone or with their Indian wives and relatives. The rendezvous combined a shopping mall and a carnival, attracting area Indian residents

Annually for Jim Bridger's birthday—on March 17—modern-day mountain men gather at Fort Bridger to celebrate. Here, Matt Bond practices his hatchet-throwing.
FRED PFLUGHOFT

along with mountain men. The largest encampment was said to have had more than a thousand people, about one-fifth the size of St. Louis in those days.

Trappers brought their "plews" (beaver skins), and Ashley's men valued each by size and

quality, tying them up in batches, "packs," of a hundred plews. The thickest, richest furs occurred when the animals needed winter warmth, so summer was perfect for getting business done.

It was all because stylish European men and women wanted fur coats and hats, waterproof fur-felt hats, and garment trims of fur. (Almost all fur from the United States was exported to Europe at the time.) For fifty years, starting around 1800, the favored material was beaver fur, from animals found in huge numbers in the Northern Rockies' cold streams. Then beaver became scarce, having been "trapped out" in many areas. Silk hats for gentlemen came into style, the stylish fur was now seal, and fine woolen cloth was exported from Great Britain, while long-term war in Europe cut into the numbers of affluent shoppers.

Before the beaver was driven extinct, the industry itself began to fade away, and beaver populations began to rebound even though some men still trapped them. Those men were no longer the only whites in the country. Wagon trains carrying men, women and children now passed through, heading for the Oregon land along a trail that Native Americans and mountain men had worn beside the Green River.

After Ashley stopped holding the Green River rendezvous, even Jim Bridger settled down—for a while at least.

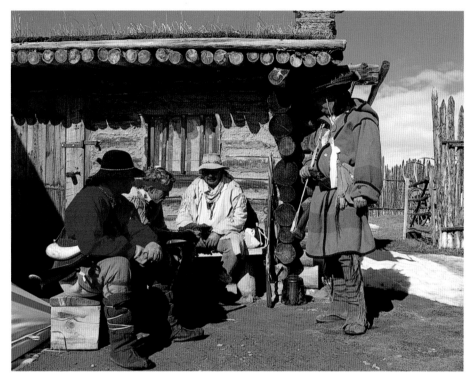

Fur trappers either traded with Indians for garments, or made their own from the materials at hand: hides, fur, and trade blankets. FRED PFLUGHOFT

December 1842, and the post opened for business in the new year. After trading with area Shoshones and Utes for furs gathered over the winter, Vasquez hurried over to Fort Laramie early each year. He was back with goods the furs paid for, and had Fort Bridger shelves stocked, before the year's first wagon train arrived. Besides offering staple goods and repairs, the partners bought pioneers' exhausted livestock and sold them fresh animals. After a season of grazing the area's nutritious grasses, the refreshed stock were offered to next year's travelers.

In 1846, Louis Vasquez married, and brought his Kentucky-born wife, Narcissa, to live at Fort Bridger in the enclave that included the Bridger family.

tle over a hundred miles downhill from the mountain crossing of South Pass. The two men figured that trains would be ready to stop to fix wagons and resupply right here, roughly the halfway point between Independence and The Dalles, Oregon, or Fort Vancouver, Washington. Bridger, an apprentice blacksmith in his youth, included a blacksmith shop and a stock of iron for repairs.

The first buildings were ready by

Right: "Mountain man"Craig Heiny, dressed in his coat made from a Hudson's Bay Company trade blanket, starts a fire without matches, in the trading post reconstruction. FRED PFLUGHOFT

Below: Michael "Bad Hand" Terry demonstrates aspects of Indian culture at the time of early white contact, such as that at Fort Bridger. FRED PFLUGHOFT

The original Fort Bridger lasted from 1842 until it was burned down in 1857. FRED PFLUGHOFT

Beginning in 1847, Fort Bridger saw the passage of Mormons, members of the Church of Jesus Christ of Latter-day Saints, intent on moving away from communities that had persecuted them because of their new faith. That year, Brigham Young, the forty-six-year-old head of the church, led the Pioneer Train of 148 people in wagons, followed by another 1,500 emigrants herding 3,500 cattle. To get to Fort Laramie in eastern Wyoming without bumping into Missourians (some of whom had persecuted them), they traveled along the north side of the Platte, across the river from the Oregon Trail. Their route came to be called the Mormon Trail. At Fort Laramie, it joined the Oregon Trail to travel across Wyoming.

Jim Bridger warned Brigham Young that the route he planned to follow led to more mountains. Young thought mountain barriers would help protect his people, and his Pioneer Train continued into territory unknown to them. Upon seeing the Great Salt Lake—which Bridger had mistaken for the Pacific Ocean twenty-two years before—Young announced, "This is the place." The Pioneer Train voted its agree-

Oxen, like those on this Mormon emigrant train, could be replaced at posts like Fort Bridger;
fattened up on wild grasses, they would be sold to another outfit the following year.
UTAH STATE HISTORICAL SOCIETY

In the top picture, modern reenactors enjoy good weather by opening up the canvas top on their Conestoga wagon. In the historical sketch at right, trail dust is probably why some of the wagons are closed as tightly as possible. UTAH STATE HISTORICAL SOCIETY

After Mormons burned the original Fort Bridger so it couldn't benefit the U.S. Army, two companies of Colonel Johnston's troops spent a miserable winter of 1857-1858 in tents on the site. At top is how Harper's Weekly portrayed the camp, and below is the sketch sent to competing Frank Leslie's Illustrated Newspaper by someone who said that Harper's pictures were "grossly incorrect" and that his drawings "represent the fort as it is, and not as it is supposed to be." BOTH IMAGES FROM UTAH STATE HISTORICAL SOCIETY

ment. Now, volunteers went back to create stations along the route to assist the 12,000 Mormons then waiting in western Iowa and eastern Nebraska. Among future Mormon emigrants would be nearly 3,000 who propelled wooden handcarts across prairie and mountain to their new home. Mormon migrations continued through Fort Bridger into the early 1860s.

One community of Mormons began Wyoming's first farming town, Willow Creek, a dozen miles away from Fort Bridger.

Although both Bridger and Vasquez once had been mountain men living the rough life of isolation punctuated by incredible partying at the rendezvous, Vasquez got along well with the Mormons. In fact, he opened a store in Salt Lake City in 1849. Bridger, however, often disagreed with Mormon leaders, and claimed their nearby trading post drove him out of the business. The Mormons countered that Bridger didn't always clear the brands of livestock he traded—meaning he didn't check to see whether they had been stolen. Bridger sold his interest in Fort Bridger in 1853 and returned to guiding. Only two years later, Louis and Narcissa Vasquez had had enough of the frontier, and sold the fort to area Mormons. The couple moved to the St. Louis area and then settled in Westport.

In 1857-1858 came the Utah—sometimes called Mormon—War, when President James Buchanan sent about one third of the U.S. Army to oust Brigham Young from his

Mormons called their first Wyoming settlement—near Fort Bridger—Fort Supply. Jim Bridger said their business drove him out of his. *UTAH STATE HISTORICAL SOCIETY*

Mormon emigrants began to pass through Wyoming, and some settled near Fort Bridger, beginning in 1847. William Henry Jackson sketched a "hand-cart company" in which most members walked from Missouri to Utah. *WYOMING STATE ARCHIVES*

In 1858, the U.S. Army built sturdy new buildings at its Fort Bridger on the former site of Fort Bridger trading post. UTAH STATE HISTORICAL SOCIETY

appointed position as governor of Utah Territory, which had been created in 1851. Young, also still head of his church, organized his own army and announced a defensive scorched-earth policy for eastern Utah. Fort Bridger was one of the places burned down so that the U.S. Army couldn't use it.

U.S. troops headed for Utah didn't leave Fort Leavenworth until mid-July 1857. Traveling the Oregon Trail, they reached the Rockies in November, too late to cross the mountain passes into Utah. Jim Bridger was on hand, eager to guide Colonel Albert Sidney Johnston's troops to the Mormons.

But in the frigid cold and massive snowstorms, supplied with too few rations, Colonel Johnston and his command wintered uncomfortably at the ruins of Fort Bridger; hundreds of men deserted.

Without full-fledged war, the incident wound down beginning in April 1858, when Brigham Young stepped down from the governorship and President Buchanan pardoned the citizens of Utah for their "rebellion." That same year, the army purchased and rebuilt Fort Bridger. During the Civil War it sometimes went unmanned, but troops always returned when available.

After the war came the great race to build the first transcontinental railroad (see the Fort Steele chapter), which passed nearby. Fort Bridger troops guarded from Indian attack Union Pacific Railroad crews, who built westward through the area in October and November 1868. When the Union Pacific met the Central Pacific Railroad at Promontory Summit, Utah, the following May, the clang of a sledge hammer on the symbolic last spike rang the death knell for covered-wagon trains.

Fort Bridger troops in the 1870s participated in Red Cloud's War and the Great Sioux Campaign, but again the fort sat empty from time to time. In 1890, the army moved out and auctioned some buildings, leaving others to ruin. Eventually, Wyoming associations and residents mounted a campaign to save the historic relic. In 1933, Fort Bridger became a Wyoming Historical Landmark; today it is a designated Wyoming State Historic Site whose grounds are open year 'round. The museum is open daily from the beginning of May to the end of September, with costumed interpreters and living history events bringing soldiers, fur traders, and overland emigrants back into Fort Bridger.

The Bachelor Officers' Quarters (above and below), while not too cozy, were far more comfortable than the barracks that housed enlisted men.

The Commanding Officer's Quarters, built in 1884, features up-to-the-minute multi-colored painted trim. FRED PFLUGHOFT

As in many a modern home, the commanding officer's hunting trophies found their place in his personal den. *DAVID M. MORRIS*

In Fort Bridger's reconstructed Commanding Officer's quarters, visitors get a sense of the lives of a frontier officer and his family in the mid-1880s. Top: In the kitchen, the pierced-tin doors of the food-safe (left wall) kept flies off baked goods and cooked meats. Below: The view from the formal parlor to the dining room shows elegantly proportioned rooms with gracious furnishings—but it was spartan living by upper middle-class standards of the day. *BOTH IMAGES BY DAVID M. MORRIS*

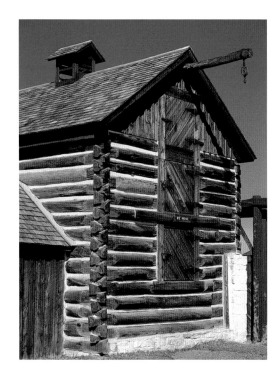

Having ice in warm months meant cutting blocks from frozen streams during winter and freighting them here to the ice house, using the block and tackle above the door to lift them inside. Packing of straw and sawdust, plus thick log walls, minimized melting to preserve the precious substance.
FRED PFLUGHOFT

Inside the Post Trader's Store during Fort Bridger's military days, one could buy crackers or pickles from a barrel, choose from a small selection of canned goods, or while away some time over the checkerboard.
DAVID M. MORRIS

The Post Trader's complex at Fort Bridger during its military days was private property. Judge William Alexander, sutler from 1857 to 1881, ran the store, butcher shop, and icehouse here. With six children of his own, he also included a schoolhouse—the first building in future Wyoming that was exclusively a school. FRED PFLUGHOFT

If you were a student at the military fort's schoolhouse in the 1870s, how many stars were on the flag you saluted?
DAVID M. MORRIS

Sited conveniently near the ice house was the post sutler's butcher shop, for those who could buy fresh meat rather than having to get along on army rations. FRED PFLUGHOFT

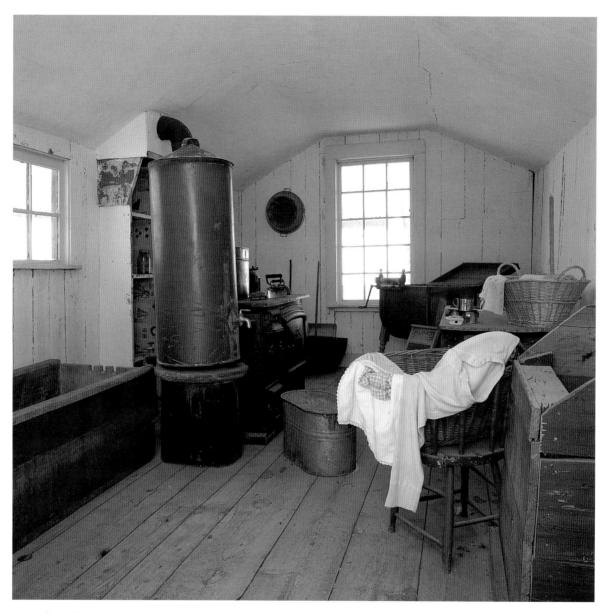

The Wash House includes a wood-fed hot-water tank and a hand cranked washing machine (back corner) complete with wringer. Often, enlisted men's wives worked as laundresses to supplement their husbands' low pay.
DAVID M. MORRIS

Above: Unidentified officers pose outside the Officers' Quarters in 1868. UNION PACIFIC HISTORICAL COLLECTION

Right: The Officers' Quarter's, shown reconstructed here, used log walls for insultation from heat and cold. FRED PFLUGHOFT

Fort Washakie
est. 1868

Chief Washakie. *WYOMING STATE ARCHIVES*

*T*he town of Fort Washakie, headquarters of the Wind River Indian Reservation, contains a still-living fort, one built to serve the eastern Shoshone Indians—a fort whose name honors a historic Shoshone leader, Chief Washakie. Its actual buildings have been remodeled into tribal offices.

Born of a Lemhi Shoshone mother and a Flathead father around 1804, the future chief lived with the Lemhi after a Blackfeet raid destroyed his father's village and left the father dead. Washakie stayed with the Lemhi after his mother moved back among the Flatheads, and then he lived for five years with the Bannocks before coming to live permanently with the eastern Shoshone.

The Bannocks fought whites encroaching into their land, and Washakie became a good warrior. Two possible translations of this name point to his prowess in battle, one being "Shoots-on-the-Run." The other, "The Rattle," refers to the story that he made an extra-large rattle of stones inside buffalo hide, which he used to scare horses of enemy Crow, Sioux, and Arapaho warriors in battle.

Washakie was tall, strong both in body and personality, and thoughtful rather than impulsive. He spoke well in presenting his ideas at councils, and was honorable in dealings with all people. In 1843, the eastern Shoshone named him their chief, which he remained until his death in 1900.

As chief, he urged his people not to attack whites coming into or passing through their lands, but rather seek to ally their relatively small band with the whites for both peace and aid against

Indian enemies. The Shoshones lived west of South Pass, and mostly allowed emigrant wagon trains pass through unharmed.

When Chief Washakie was in his mid- to late fifties, however, warriors who disagreed with his peace policy began attacking travelers on the Overland Trail. After four years, some of them were killed by Colonel Patrick E. Connor's troops in the Battle of Bear River early in 1863. That defeat raised Washakie's reputation among his people once again.

At Fort Bridger that same summer, the eastern Shoshone negotiated a treaty with the U.S. government. For allowing wagon trains to pass freely, they would receive cash payments and annuities of manufactured goods and staple foods, for twenty years.

Five years later, again at Fort Bridger, Chief Washakie and his people worked out terms for their present home n the Wind River Valley, a favorite area they called "Warm Valley." Fort Brown, built as reservation headquarters, soon was renamed Fort Washakie. When, in 1896, the Shoshone ceded reservation land around hot springs near Thermopolis, Chief Washakie specified that some of the healing mineral water must always be available, for free, to people of all races.

Shoshones gather at Fort Washakie for the distribution of annuities around 1885. WYOMING STATE ARCHIVES

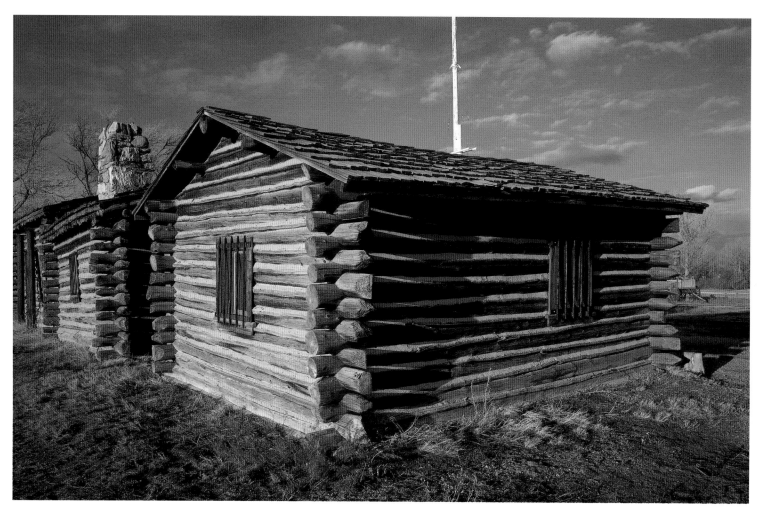

From historical sketches of Fort Caspar's long-gone structures, the buildings were reconstructed in 1936 as they had looked in 1865. FRED PFLUGHOFT

FORT CASPAR

EST. 1862

Poor Fort Caspar! It had a brief life, and then was torn down and carted away to be recycled into another military post. But it stirred the hearts and memories of the neighbors, and at last they brought it back to life. Today Fort Caspar fascinates and educates visitors by taking them back to the 19th century frontier.

In a way, it started with a ferry. In 1847, Brigham Young led the Pioneer Party of Mormons, the advance group looking for a place where members of the Church of Jesus Christ of Latter-day Saints could settle without persecution. As soon as the site of Salt Lake City was chosen, volunteers set up stations along the route to help fellow Mormons heading to future Utah during the 1850s and 1860s. Some of these volunteers built and ran Mormon Ferry across the North Platte River right where Fort Caspar would stand; later

they moved the ferry a few miles east. The ferry was free for church members but any emigrant could use it for a fee, to get a wagon across the river in five minutes without endangering people, and household goods by driving through the water. The Mormons also opened a post where emigrants could buy supplies and staple goods they'd run out of.

In 1852, John Baptiste Richard built a toll bridge a little bit east of the second Mormon Ferry location. Richard also had a trading post handy for those needing to stock up. Eighteen fifty-two was the peak of travel on the Oregon/California/Mormon Trail to South Pass, when 50,000 emigrants used it. Since crossing Richard's bridge took even less time than using the Mormon or other ferries, travelers gladly paid to drive across the span. Richard prospered, and even put the ferry out of business.

The U.S. Army, to protect emigrant trains, manned garrisons near the bridge in 1855-1856 (Fort Clay, renamed Camp Davis) and again in 1858-1859 (Post at Platte Bridge, commonly called Camp Payne).

But in only eight years, Richard's bridge lost its advantage. Louis Guinard built a newer and better bridge (and his own trading post at its south side) at the future site of Fort Caspar; it opened in the spring of 1860. Some emigrants had settled around Richard's bridge and post, and now some more stopped off around Guinard's. Area population was growing.

The Pony Express began that same year, and selected Guinard's post as the site of one of its relay stations; later, the Overland Mail Company operated its own station here. When the transcontinental telegraph line went through this area, it crossed the North Platte literally on Guinard's bridge, and his trading post now included a Pacific Telegraph Company office. The first telegraph message that went from California nonstop across the continent was sent on October 24, 1861, assuring President Abraham Lincoln that Californians remained loyal to the Union.

With the Civil War on, military and gov-

Above: William Henry Jackson, later known as a photographer of the West, drove a freight wagon west in 1866. His painting of Guinard's Bridge shows how substantially Louis Guinard built the second bridge at the future Fort Caspar site. This work is on exhibit at Fort Caspar today. *WYOMING STATE ARCHIVES*

Left: Visitors get a sense of Guinard's Bridge from this reconstructed segment. *FRED PFLUGHOFT*

Buffalo Bill

William F. Cody at twenty-four, ten years after his record-breaking Pony Express ride. By now he held the nickname "Buffalo Bill" after a two-year contract of shooting bison to feed builders of the Union Pacific, and was halfway through a four-year hitch as scout for the 5th U.S. Cavalry.
WYOMING STATE ARCHIVES

*W*illiam Frederick Cody, who had ongoing ties to Wyoming, has become such a figure of legend that it can be hard to recall his real deeds. As an intelligent but undereducated man, he did what he could to make a living; because that included his hugely successful wild west show during the heyday of traveling circuses, he is remembered as much as a showman as for his frontier work.

Born in 1846 to a Union sympathizer in Iowa, Bill was the middle of seven children who attended frontier schools as they were available. His politically active father took the family to Kansas Territory as soon as it was opened to homesteaders in 1854. When the senior Cody died only three years later, Bill was nine years old, but that marked the end of the boy's formal education.

Bill went to work as a horseback messenger for the Leavenworth office of Majors and Russell. In 1861, when the company was Russell, Majors and Waddell and Bill was fourteen, he worked for them as a Pony Express rider. In between those jobs, he'd been a wagon train bullwhacker and had taken part in the Pikes Peak gold rush. Sharing his father's Unionist sympathies, Cody enlisted in a Kansas volunteer cavalry company, serving nineteen months that included a year's active service in the Civil War, where he was commended for excellent marksmanship.

Cody's military service was all with the rank of an enlisted man, but in 1887 the governor of Nebraska, former Wyoming Territory governor John Thayer, named Cody an aide-de-camp to his staff, with the rank of colonel. From then on, Buffalo Bill was pleased to be called Colonel Cody.

At the ripe old age of twenty, he married Louisa Frederici, whom he'd met while posted to St. Louis in the cavalry. Within the year their first child, a daughter named Arta, was born.

During 1867-1868, Cody supported his family by working for the Union Pacific railroad as a meat hunter for crews building across Wyoming. Like the Plains Indians who depended on the bison, Cody killed only as many animals as were needed. That's when he earned the nickname "Buffalo Bill." He never participated, however, in the later wholesale bison slaughter by hide hunters and sport shooters who wasted the meat. In fact, the bison herd Cody maintained for his traveling show helped preserve the species during its ebb years in the 1880s and 1890s.

When General Phil Sheridan heard that Cody willingly carried dispatches through areas controlled by hostile Indians, he hired the young man as a cavalry scout. Although most such civilian employees worked by contract for a month at a time, or for a specific military campaign, Cody set a record by scouting continuously for more than four years, from 1868 into 1872. He was awarded the Medal of Honor for his action during an 1872 Indian fight in Nebraska, but it was rescinded forty-four years later because he had been a civilian and the medal was for military men only.

The legend of Buffalo Bill began in 1869, when "Ned Buntline" (Edward Judson) published a dime novel called Buffalo Bill, the King of Border Men. Colorful adventure novelettes that sold for ten cents apiece, dime novels were the pulp fiction of their day. The Buffalo

Bill "autobiography" was such a success that Buntline wrote a stage melodrama about the character and, in 1872, talked Cody into appearing as himself during some Chicago performances.

From that time both the man and the legend progressed through life, each with growing success. Cody spent winters performing in theaters, and summers guiding for the military or such figures as Russia's Grand Duke Alexis. When in army employ earlier, Cody had fought in sixteen Indian battles, but his most famous became one against the Cheyenne in 1876, a month after the Cheyenne and Sioux defeated George Custer at the Little Bighorn. Cody killed the warrior Yellow Hair, an act trumpeted in national newspapers as "the first scalp for Custer."

Still, Cody respected the one-time foes, and joined a small minority of American voices speaking on behalf of just treatment and civil rights for Native Americans three years later. And, in 1885, he explained: "The defeat of Custer was not a massacre. The Indians were being pursued by skilled fighters with orders to kill. For centuries they had been hounded from the Atlantic to the Pacific and back again. They had their wives and little ones to protect and they were fighting for their existence."

In 1883, Cody created his great traveling show, Buffalo Bill's Wild West Show and Congress of Rough Riders, which delivered past and passing aspects of the American West by train around the nation for thirty years, and by ship to Europe in 1887, 1889-1893, and 1903-1907.

With horses, cattle and bison, stagecoaches, buckboards, and "Roman chariots" careening around the arena while plenty of blank bullets went off, Cody's wild west show became the leader of its type. Acts included an Overland Stage robbery, reenactments of famous Indian battles, the choreographed changing of Pony Express riders, and cowboys on bucking broncos. Skilled shooters performed tricks designed to impress audiences filled with people who handled guns and hunted frequently—but could they shoot a cigarette from their spouse's lips, as Annie Oakley could? Indians were part of the company, treated respectfully by Cody and their co-performers (if not by every audience), and for part of the 1885 tour, Cody even convinced Chief Sitting Bull, a Sioux leader at Little Bighorn, to go along. The chief became friends with Oakley and her husband, sharpshooter Frank Butler.

Meanwhile, Louisa and Bill's family had grown, with Arta followed by their only son and namesake of a fellow scout, Kit Carson Cody (1870), and sisters Orra (1872), and Irma Louise (1883). Sadly, Kit died in 1876, and Orra in 1883. Even Arta, dying in 1904, did not outlive her parents.

Dime novels with Cody's byline continued to pour onto the market, along with many "autobiographies" by various authors, but not Buffalo Bill himself.

In his fifties, with the Wild West Show well established but always financially shaky, Cody began to diversity his investments, joining many projects in Wyoming, among other Western states. He developed land in the Big Hole Basin, where he also built irrigation systems. As a frequent guest and part owner of the Sheridan's Sheridan Inn, he was known to settle on the building's large veranda to audition acts for the wild west show. He was among the founders, at the turn of the twentieth century, of the town of Shoshone—soon renamed Cody. There, in

1902, he built a sandstone hotel named for daughter Irma; its rooms and restaurant continue to welcome guests today, and the Irma is listed on the National Register of Historical Places. Near Yellowstone National Park, he built his hunting lodge of Pahaska Teepee.

The Irma Hotel in Cody still serves the public. FRED PFLUGHOFT

In 1913, when traveling tent shows were merging in order to stay alive, Buffalo Bill's Wild West Show was seized and sold at auction for a loan payment that the cash-poor showman couldn't meet. No problem—Cody thought he'd now start making moving picture shows about the Indian wars. And when he died, four years later, he probably still had plenty of ideas for new projects.

Left: A fife and drum corps participates in the biennial Platte Bridge Station reenactment at Fort Caspar.
FRED PFLUGHOFT

Below: Not visiting Fort Caspar until the year after the Battle of Platte Bridge, William Henry Jackson must have sketched this view of it from eyewitness accounts.
WYOMING STATE ARCHIVES

ernment use of the telegraph line took priority over civilian messages. The Union government didn't take over the telegraph, though, because private businesses' communications with the gold-rich land on the Pacific Coast also were important for the nation. In June 1862, when soldiers were needed for battles in the East, the army sent four companies of the 6th Ohio Volunteer Cavalry here to guard the telegraph line and the mail service. Their garrison near Guinard's bridge was called simply Platte Bridge Station, and the men were commanded from Fort Laramie by Lieutenant Colonel William O. Collins. Fort Collins, Colorado had been named for him.

Indians who lived in the area understood how important the telegraph lines and the mail were to the whites intruding into their land, so part of their warfare was to cut the wires and attack mail carriers. It even fell to Collins' soldiers to repair downed telegraph lines.

Added to the soldiers at Platte Bridge Station, beginning in 1864, were some "galvanized Yankees," the name given to Confederate prisoners of war who enlisted in the Union army and served on the western frontier.

At the end of November 1864, in Colorado Territory, an event occurred that would affect Indians and whites on the northern plains for years to come. Black Kettle's band of Cheyennes were asleep in their camp on Sand Creek, where a truce flag flew; they believed they were at peace with the U.S. Army. At dawn, a thousand Colorado militia led by Colonel John Chivington attacked the camp under order to take no prisoners, killing at least 200 Cheyennes (mostly women and children) and mutilating their bodies. The Union reacted in horror, as did the Cheyennes and other Indian peoples they carried the news to during that winter.

Spring and summer 1865 brought Cheyenne and Sioux attacks in retribution for the Sand Creek Massacre, and heightened alertness among frontier military troops. Passing through Platte Bridge Station to his post at Sweetwater Station was Lieutenant Caspar Collins, the colonel's son. On July 26, the lieutenant led a unit to meet and escort a supply train that was coming in from Sweetwater. Cheyenne warriors led by Roman Nose, and Sioux warriors under Red Cloud, attacked the soldiers when they had traveled only a mile, and Lieutenant Collins was killed in what is called the Battle of Platte Bridge. When the supply train appeared in the distance, the Indians also attacked it and killed all but three of its men, in the Battle of Red Buttes.

Four months later, the army changed the name of Platte Bridge Station to Fort Caspar, in honor of young Collins. In 1888, with its spelling altered, his name would be taken by the community that was growing about four miles away.

More troops were added to Fort Caspar's roster in 1866, but the following year the fort suddenly was no longer important. The Union Pacific's arrival at Cheyenne, to the south, meant that mail could travel that far by train—and the line was being built rapidly westward. The Oregon Trail, and forts protecting it, were on their way to becoming history.

As Fort Caspar did in 1867. Its troops were ordered to the new Fort Fetterman on the Bozeman Trail, and told to take all materials and items that would be of use there, including Fort Caspar's buildings. The empty site was part of CY Ranch holdings by the 1880s.

But residents of the city of Casper and surrounding Natrona County didn't forget about the fort, and the city bought eighty acres that included its site in 1922. In 1933, the first replica Fort Caspar was built there, based on floor plans sketched by Caspar Collins himself. During a reenactment that year of the Battle of Platte Bridge, though, flaming arrows did just what they were designed to, and burned down the replica. What visitors see today was built in 1936; the City of Casper obtained matching funds from the Works Progress Administration. Furnishings, gear, and uniforms represent Fort Caspar in 1865.

The Interpretive Center that opened in 1983 holds changing exhibits that include all aspects of area history from Paleo Indian culture to Plains Indians and on to Fort Caspar's heyday. Outdoors, reproductions show the Mormon Ferry and part of Guinard's bridge, and signs tell of the Pony Express and Overland Mail services.

And, all summer, Fort Caspar is very much alive as volunteer reenactors tell their stories and demonstrate the work skills of nearly a century and a half ago.

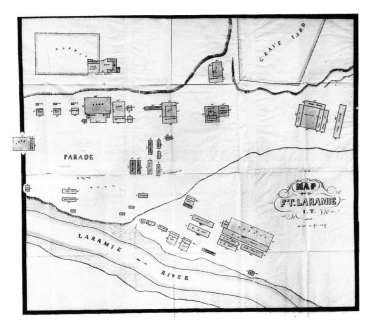

Above: Lieutenant Caspar Collins, namesake of Fort Caspar, obviously had the training of a young gentleman of his day. He painted this view of Fort Laramie when he visited there in 1865, catching such details of daily life as Indian women using a dog travois. WESTERN HISTORY DEPARTMENT, DENVER PUBLIC LIBRARY

Left: Lt. Collins also carefully drafted this schematic map of Fort Laramie, Indian Territory, in 1865. KANSAS STATE HISTORICAL SOCIETY

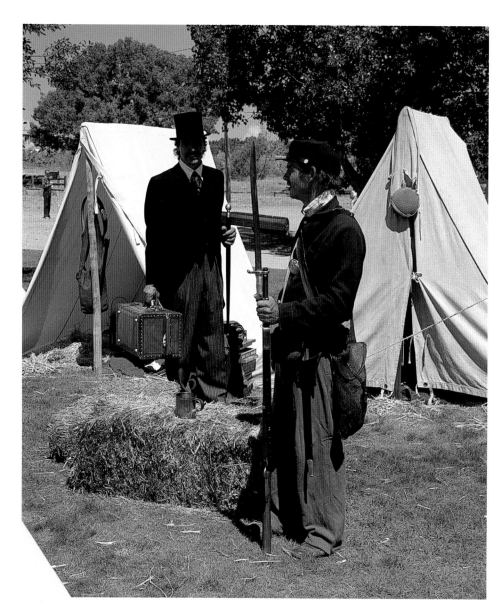

Right: The man in the natty pinstriped suit portrays a civilian doctor at Fort Caspar, carrying his medical kit that probably held his entire pharmacy.
FRED PFLUGHOFT

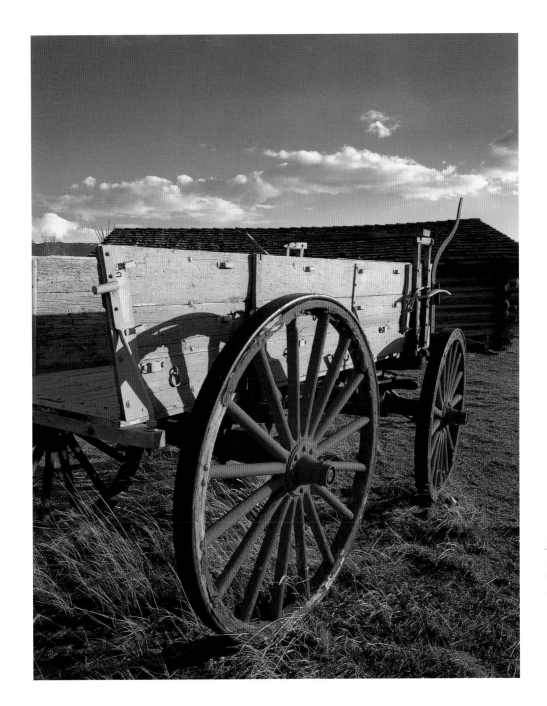

The pickup truck of the frontier was this type of light freight wagon, sometimes called a buckboard.
FRED PLUGHOFT

Below: Fort Phil Kearny was the largest of three forts built to try to protect emigrant wagon trains on the Bozeman Trail. WYOMING STATE ARCHIVES

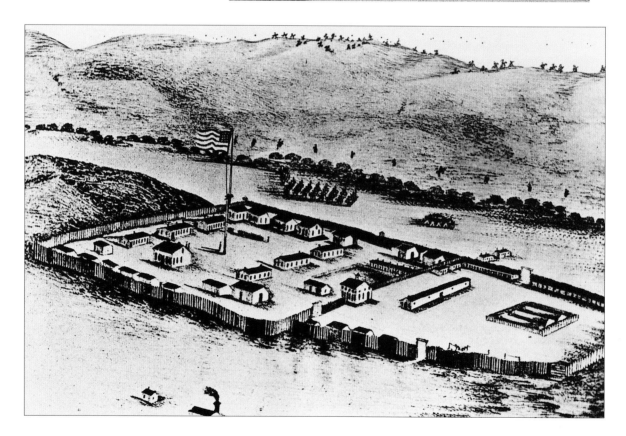

FORT PHIL KEARNY

EST. 1866

For those who wanted to reach the rich 1862 gold strike in Montana—the sooner the better, of course—the Overland Trail route was too long. John M. Bozeman and John Jacobs figured prospectors would pay to be guided on a more direct route, one that these two laid out in 1863, going northwest through Wyoming's Powder River country.

When Jim Bridger heard the plan, he was totally against it. He told his two fellow mountain men that it was a foolish route, with little forage for animals, and little water—but, even worse, it went through the center of prime Sioux hunting land. When the Sioux learned about it, their opinion was even more negative, and not expressed in mere words.

The Bozeman Trail lasted for six travel seasons, and deserved its nickname of "the bloody Bozeman."

Halfway through the trail's existence, two forts in Wyoming (and one over the line in Montana) were built to protect it. Even they failed. And John Bozeman was killed by Indians on his namesake trail the last year it was open.

The Sioux won what whites called "Red Cloud's War," the Bozeman Trail was closed, and Indians destroyed the trail's Wyoming forts.

It didn't help that two different U.S. government departments each believed that it was the one in charge of the situation. After the Civil War, the notoriously corrupt Indian Office dealt with Indians who were at peace with the United States, distributing annuities of cheap quality and pocketing the profit. These annuities included such staples as coffee, rice, dried meat and hardtack, and cloth-

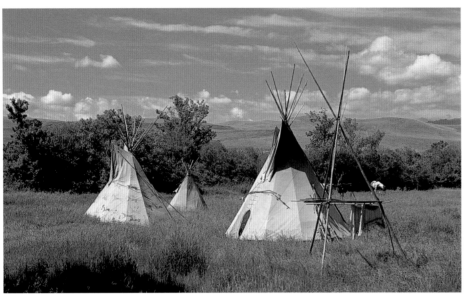

ing and bedding. They were to be given annually a the number of years—set by treaty with each tribe—to help during the transition from buffalo-hunting to self-supporting farming. Besides supplying inferior goods, some government agents failed to distribute the annuities promptly, letting them sit in storage at a fort while the rightful recipients waited in camp nearby.

But if Indians went to war, the United States War Department took over all relations with that tribe or nation. Further complicating things, both federal agencies believed that

Indian nations were organized like their own—with one leader at the top.

Take the Oglala Sioux then living in the Powder River basin of Wyoming. They had a brilliant war leader named Red Cloud. He could never become a chief himself because, more than twenty years before, he had killed a chief who was feuding with another chief, Red Cloud's uncle who raised him. Still, Red Cloud was respected and followed in battle.

In 1865, the army sent General Patrick E. Connor into the Powder River country to intimidate Sioux and Cheyenne who regularly attacked emigrant trains on the Bozeman Trail, trying to stop the whites from scaring the buffalo herds away from this rich hunting land. Connor had served in the Seminole War, the Mexican War, and (during the Civil War) in Utah, and had been a businessman between wars. His expedition, a failure, is described in the Fort Reno sidebar in this chapter.

The next year, Congress sent a peace commission to end the situation, and keep the

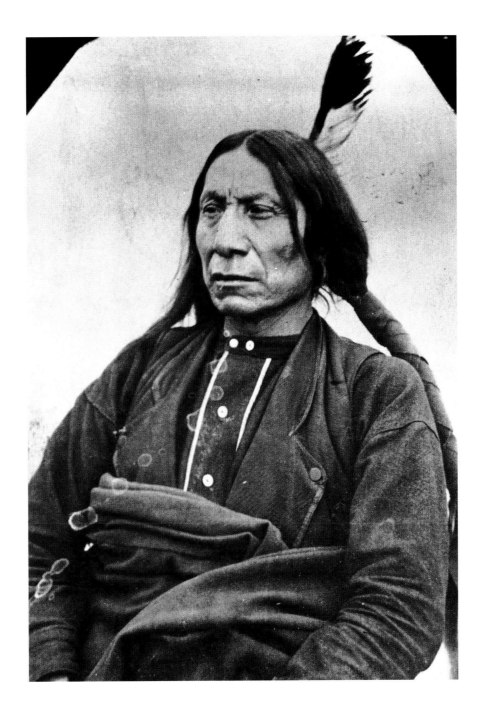

Red Cloud (ca. 1822-1907) was the Oglala Sioux military tactician who led the successful Sioux-Cheyenne-Arapaho efforts to close the Bozeman Trail, the campaign that whites would label "Red Cloud's War." WYOMING STATE ARCHIVES

Whether your team was composed of beautiful horses, stollid oxen, or cantankerous mules, the path to a better life in the Oregon country was tedious and uncomfortable, as well as dangerous.
FRED PFLUGHOFT

Colonel Henry B. Carrington to take troops into Powder River country and build forts. Carrington had served during the Civil War, recruiting and training volunteer troops, but never had seen battle.

He led his newly assigned troops westward, stopping at Fort Laramie. Just where—and when—the peace commission was meeting with the Sioux! Red Cloud and others were furious at such falseness: they thought the whites had pretended to talk peace while actually awaiting their soldiers.

Carrington moved 169 miles up the Bozeman Trail from Fort Laramie, where he had the year-old Fort Connor torn down, moved about a mile, and rebuilt as Fort Reno. Its name honored General Jesse L. Reno of the Civil War, not Marcus Reno, subordinate to George A. Custer.

Bozeman Trail safely open by treaty rather than war. They invited Sioux leaders—including the man they thought was "head chief," Red Cloud—to Fort Laramie to negotiate. While Red Cloud was willing to talk, he also thought it was obvious to all that no one man, especially himself, could speak for every Sioux.

Meanwhile that same year of 1866, the U.S. Army decided to get serious about keeping the Bozeman Trail open. They named

Right: In 1866, Colonel Henry B. Carrington was named to lead U.S. Army efforts to protect the Bozeman Trail, in part by building new forts along it. WYOMING STATE ARCHIVES

Below: Bozeman Trail Days bring back the sound of field artillery at Fort Phil Kearney. FRED PFLUGHOFT

When the frontier army was in the field, they traveled light and lived in spartan style. FRED PFLUGHOFT

Territory border, ninety-one miles north of Phil Kearny, Carrington also had Fort C.F. Smith erected along the Bozeman Trail.

Fort Phil Kearny was the largest of the three Bozeman Trail forts, and surrounded by a sturdy stockade. It became the main target of the Sioux, Cheyenne, and Arapahoes, to whom it was "hated fort."

Another sixty-seven miles north on the trail (about sixteen miles south of today's Sheridan), Carrington built Fort Phil Kearny to his own design. The fort was named for a Union general killed in the Civil War; it shouldn't be confused with another Oregon Trail military post, Fort Kearny on the Platte River in Nebraska. The later was named for Colonel S.W. Kearny, who pronounced his name *CAR-nee*. Wyoming's fort is pronounced *KERR-nee*.

On the other side of the Montana

None of the three forts was especially well situated, or well supplied with rations or even, amazingly, with ammunition. During the first winter, which happened to be extremely cold, the forts were without vegetables and fresh meat; a loaf of bread per man per day, salt pork, hardtack, and occasional bean soup filled the menu. Enlisted men considered serving at them to be hardship duty; morale was low and desertion rates were high. And highly motivated Indian adversaries were all around.

One of Fort Phil Kearny'problems was that a wood supply wasn't close at hand. To keep the fort heated and supplied with bread, a crew of soldiers had to leave the stockade and cut wood out in the open. Area Indians had observed this, and on the sub-zero, snowy day of December 21, 1866, attacked the wood train. To rescue the train, Colonel Carrington sent out Brevet Lieutenant Colonel William J. Fetterman, with nearly half the fort's garrison, eighty-one men. That was an interesting number, since Fetterman had bragged that with eighty good men he could beat all of the Sioux in existence!

Fetterman fell for a ruse created by Red Cloud. Nearing the wood train, Fetterman saw that the attacking Indian party (led by Crazy Horse) was pretty small. So, Fetterman counter-attacked. Crazy Horse led his little decoy party, and the soldiers, into a mass of from one to three thousand warriors, depending on the account. Colonel Carrington later defended himself by claiming that he hadn't told Fetterman to go that far away from the fort.

Fetterman and all his men were killed within minutes, and their bodies scalped and mutilated as the ultimate insult.

The Sioux warriors must have left the area at once, because soldiers from the fort recovered forty-nine bodies and counted thirty-two more that same day.

Inside Fort Phil Kearny were now 119 men, including civilian employees, and some women and children. Their fear was that the Sioux would return and overrun the fort.

Colonel Carrington sat down and wrote a dispatch demanding reinforcements—two companies of cavalry, or four of infantry, supplied with the new repeating rifles. Guns he'd been told left Fort Leavenworth, in Kansas, back in September hadn't arrived, he complained, and cavalry ordered to join his garrison hadn't shown up either. His men right now had only about twenty rounds of ammunition apiece. Carrington didn't ask that those at Fort Phil Kearny be saved, but instead argued that if the Sioux closed the Bozeman Trail now, it would take even more troops to reopen it when spring came.

Not to lessen his forces further (even teamsters were on duty now, and sentries had to be relieved every quarter hour in this cold), Carrington hired two civilian volunteers to deliver his request to the nearest telegraph station. John Phillips, who had immigrated from

John "Portugee" Phillips rode to Fort Laramie with word of the Fetterman Fight, hiding by day and traveling by night on December 23 through 24, 1866. WYOMING STATE ARCHIVES

Portugal, worked for the fort quartermaster and was known to all as "Portugee." Phillips' good friend, Daniel Dixon, went along; he is described only as being of "mixed blood." Colonel Carrington lent one of his own horses, which Phillips rode, for the endeavor.

Later legend-making turned Phillips into the sole rider and compared him to Paul Revere. That's reasonable, since Revere didn't ride alone, either. The true story is amazing enough without further exaggeration. We don't know whether Dixon made the entire trip, but two other riders were with Phillips for the last (but safest) leg of the journey.

The telegraph was at Horseshoe Station on the Overland Stage line, the site of today's Glendo. Besides the snow and arctic cold, no one knew where the Sioux warriors might be. Phillips and Dixon set out before midnight, planning to ride by night and hide during daylight. They were wrapped up in long coats, hats, gauntlets and boots—all made of buffalo hide. Reasoning that the Sioux would expect whites to follow the precious road that had caused all this trouble, Phillips traveled parallel to the Bozeman Trail, but as many as ten miles away from it.

According to one account, a lone Phillips

reached Fort Reno in the wee hours of the 22nd, pausing only briefly to shout the news to the sentinel before taking off at a smart trot. But according to the fort's quartermaster, two men arrived "in the early hours" exhausted from riding all night, and rested.

On the 23rd and 24th, Phillips hid in snow and brush during the nine or ten hours of daylight. Late on the 24th, Phillips ran into a group of mounted Indian warriors, but was able to race them to a hilltop and hold them off until dark fell. After keeping himself awake all night, Phillips took off at first light. He reached Horseshoe Station at 10:00 on Christmas morning, and Carrington's message was sent.

But what if he had come all that way and the weather, or Indians, had taken down the telegraph line? The lines often were down. Phillips decided to ride on to Fort Laramie. He reached there that same evening during a Christmas party at the bachelor officers' club, the building then nicknamed "Bedlam." When Phillips dismounted, his horse fell dead on the parade ground. As soon as Phillips made his way inside—his buffalo clothing covered with snow and his beard dripping icicles—and announced he had a dispatch from the embattled fort, some say he fainted away in exhaustion.

General H.W. Wessels left Fort Laramie at once with four companies of infantry and one of cavalry. Having to slog through snow that was two feet and more deep, the troops took until January 17 to reach Fort Phil Kearny. Some men were dropped off at Fort Reno along the way, suffering from frostbite that required amputations.

Until the Battle of the Little Bighorn not quite a decade later, the Fetterman Fight was the U.S. Army's worst defeat at the hands of Plains Indians. It tarnished Colonel Carrington's chances of career advancement, although he later commanded quieter posts. (Today, some historians even wonder whether Carrington falsely stated that Fetterman disobeyed orders.) General Wessels was placed in command of Fort Phil Kearny.

The Fetterman Fight also seemed to give its victors too much confidence. The Indians were quiet the rest of the hard winter, but as soon as spring weather allowed traffic on the Bozeman Trail, they went back to attacking emigrant and freight trains heading for the booming Montana gold fields, and any soldiers who ventured outside the three forts.

The following August (1867), the Indians split their force of warriors and attacked Fort C.F. Smith in Montana one day while the other half traveled south to Fort Phil Kearny for a battle the next day. How many warriors there were varies in the telling; some say 2,500 to 3,000 attacked each site, others say maybe 800 at each.

A few miles from Fort Smith, soldiers had built an encampment inside a log and brush fence, where they cut and cured hay for the fort's horses. Nineteen men stayed in tents there for the harvest, since it was too far to return to the main fort each day. They were used to being harassed by passing Sioux, but on the morning of August 1 they found themselves under full-scale attack. Two men were killed at once, and four men wounded (one of them died later). Of the camp's twenty-nine mules and two horses, only one mule and one horse survived. Flaming arrows shot into the fence were extinguished, and dry grass set aflame on three sides of the camp did not smoke the soldiers out. The battle, now known as the Hayfield Fight, lasted from 9 a.m. to 5 p.m. before the Indians withdrew. (The site is now on private property.)

On August 2, the other large group of Sioux, Cheyenne, and Arapaho warriors reached the area of Fort Phil Kearny. As with the Fetterman Fight, they attacked wood cutters, but things didn't go as they had the previous December.

In June that year, a bull train run by private contractors had brought Fort Phil Kearny wagons full of rations and forage—and the promised rifles, with plenty of ammunition. Now these frontier soldiers had modern breech-loading rifles to replace their old muzzleloaders. The freighters contracted to cut wood for the coming winter, which meant there'd be no more vulnerable wood trains like Fetterman had sought to rescue.

Near today's town of Story early in July, the freighters set up their encampment near separate sites where they'd cut wood. They took the boxes off fourteen of their and the fort's plain wooden wagons, and used them to form an oval corral for their oxen. It had openings that a man, but not a beast, could pass through. A wagon box with its canvas still on, and two complete wagons, stored supplies and rations.

One company of Fort Phil Kearny soldiers was assigned to protect the wood-cutting bullwhackers for a month at a time. All the men pitched their tents just outside the wagon-box corral. In case of Indian attack, everyone was to run from the cutting sites into the corral. Because of that unusual structure, the battle that raged here on August 2, 1867, is known as the Wagon Box Fight.

The month of July had been quiet, and just the day before, a new company of soldiers had replaced the first ones. They didn't know that Indians, including war leader Red Cloud, watched the exchange from up in the hills.

After breakfast on the 2nd, a wagon train loaded with logs, escorted by twenty soldiers, headed for Fort Phil Kearny. Seven or eight wagons, with an escort of thirteen men, headed to a cutting site about 1,200 yards from the corral. Suddenly Indians seemed to be everywhere. Soldiers and freighters, firing as they went, made their way toward the corral amid arrows, and bullets from the Indians' muzzleloaders. Twenty-six soldiers and six bullwhackers made it into the corral. In command of the group, Captain James Powell gave only one order: "Shoot to kill." After the soldiers' first round of firing, Indians advanced boldly, expecting the men

Exhibits at Fort Phil Kearny State Historic Site include artifacts from the way of life local indians were trying to protect by closing the Bozeman Trail. FRED PFLUGHOFT

to draw their ramrods and take thirty seconds to reload—that's how the muzzleloading guns worked. Instead, with the new guns, the soldiers quickly loaded cartridges into the breeches of their weapons, and fired nearly continuously.

Indians who were on horseback, and many on foot and armed with arrows and spears, attacked and withdrew in waves. The day was intensely hot, but the soldiers took off their caps to carry and hold bullets. They drank old coffee and water heated by the sun. Flaming arrows set fire to ox manure inside

the corral, creating acrid smoke. Indians signaled among themselves with pocket mirrors reflecting sunlight. Bullets and arrowheads shredded the flimsy wooden wagon boxes, the soldiers' only protection.

At about three o'clock in the afternoon, as warriors on horseback stayed in the background, the soldiers heard an "awful humming, chanting sound" that grew in volume until they saw a wedge formation of hundreds of Indians, on foot, running up a ravine toward the corral. Soldiers fired a constant volley into the group, but even as individuals fell the mass of men advanced. Just when it seemed that momentum alone would carry

warriors over the wagon box barriers, the formation broke up and its members fled.

As the stunned soldiers sat in relative silence, they heard reinforcements from Fort Phil Kearny approaching, firing a brass cannon. Indians began to move out. Three men had been killed, and two wounded, inside the makeshift corral.

Almost exactly a year later, the army abandoned Fort Phil Kearny, along with Reno and C.F. Smith. Many factors had combined: the regular Indian attacks, a need to move army troops to the South as part of Reconstruction, peace advocates' work against war on Indians, and the railroad. With

When these men completed their agreement at Fort Laramie in 1868, the Bozeman Trail was closed and its forts abandoned, to the delight of the victorious Sioux.
WYOMING STATE ARCHIVES

the Union Pacific Railroad completed to central Wyoming, the Bozeman Trail no longer was the fastest way to Montana gold camps. Whites no longer cared about the road that had taken so many lives.

Shortly after troops pulled out in August 1868, the Cheyenne burned the "hated fort" to the ground. In 1963, the remains were designated a National Historic Landmark.

Today, Fort Phil Kearny State Historic Site offers self-guided tours among the building locations, and an interpretive center with exhibits and videos. In a Civilian Conservation Corps cabin dating from the 1930s, artifacts portray the quarters of an officer's wife and of a non-commissioned officer.

Walking tours of the nearby Fetterman Fight and Wagon Box Fight sites take visitors among interpretive signs that portray the battles in detail, as experienced by both Indian and white participants.

Bozeman Trail Days at the end of June brings living history interpreters and the public together at Fort Phil Kearny, with representatives of area Native Americans, mountain men, frontier artillery, cavalry and infantry men, and wagon-train emigrants.

Fort Reno

est. 1865

*H*idden Indian warriors who watched the first batch of soldiers sent to chase them out of their prime buffalo-hunting land must have laughed at the spectacle. Some of the bluecoats got lost and roamed around starving—until their own Indian scouts rescued them.

General Patrick E. Connor led the first Powder River Expedition up the Bozeman Trail in 1865, and everything went wrong. At the last minute, the army canceled its plan to give him more troops. The enlisted men, and their officers, didn't know the country, and their maps were poor. There wasn't enough food, ammunition, or equipment. And then General Connor made some bad decisions.

He divided his men into three columns, and marched his own group north from Fort Laramie. After leaving some men to build Fort Connor on the Powder River—halfway point of Wyoming's part of the Bozeman Trail—he moved up near today's Ranchester. There he attacked a village of Arapaho Indians, people who had been staying out of the conflict between the Sioux and the army. After that, angry Arapahos joined the Sioux and Cheyenne.

Connor's second column had marched from Omaha into the Black Hills, where it joined the third column, which had come from Fort Laramie. The larger group headed northwest toward Montana, to meet Connor's own column on the Rosebud River.

They didn't make it. They were able to fight off Indian attacks, but they ran out of supplies and became lost. Finally, Connor sent out some of his Pawnee scouts, who found the two lost columns and took them to Fort Connor.

That was all in 1865. The next year, Connor left the army, and Fort Connor was torn down, moved closer to the Bozeman Trail, rebuilt, and named Fort Reno.

The men who constructed and garrisoned the fort were mostly "galvanized Yankees," who found life at Fort Reno grim but relatively safe: Indians attacked it only once. During the summer travel seasons in 1866 and 1867, wagon trains were escorted from here to Fort Phil Kearny. If a train had too few wagons, soldiers had to force the eager emigrants to stay at Fort Reno until other travelers came along. The mail came up from Fort Laramie once a week.

In 1866, Nelson Story drove the first herd of cattle along the Bozeman Trail into Montana. Ten miles south of Fort Reno, Indians attacked and wounded Story's trail boss and another man. Cowboys rode to the fort to get an ambulance for the men, who were left at Reno to recover. After taking a brief rest at Reno, the trail drive moved on. Just before Christmas of that year, John "Portugee" Phillips stopped here for a little rest and some supplies on his dash to Fort Laramie with news of the Fetterman Battle.

Then, early in August 1868, Fort Reno's short life was over. The last emigrant wagon train had passed by in July. The Bozeman Trail was closed, and the fort abandoned. Victorious Indians burned it down.

Today, nothing is left of the Bozeman Trail's first fort, and its empty site in Johnson County is difficult to find.

Fort Fetterman's recon-structed Officer's Quarters now houses a museum.
FRED PFLUGHOFT

Officers of the 3rd and 4th Infantry pose at the Fort Fetterman buildings their men con-structed. WYOMING STATE ARCHIVES

FORT FETTERMAN

EST. 1867

For a frontier army soldier, being assigned to any of Wyoming's Bozeman Trail forts (Fetterman, Reno, and Phil Kearny) was hardship duty, but being assigned to Fort Fetterman was considered punishment. The site was hotter than one version of Hades in summer, and colder than the other version in winter.

Fort Fetterman was built by four companies of infantry in the summer of 1867, above the North Platte River Valley, where the Bozeman Trail turned north from the Oregon Trail. Many of the buildings, including the post hospital, had stood at Fort Caspar, then were torn down and rebuilt here. (For the story of this fort's ill-fated namesake, William J. Fetterman, see the Bozeman Trail chapter.) The builders' commander, Major William McEnery Dye, thought the location a good one because it wasn't low enough to be flooded and not high enough to be affected by winter winds.

But when Lieutenant Colonel H.W. Wessels came to take command of the fort in November of that year, he found the men miserably sheltered "under canvas exposed on a bleak plain to violent and almost constant gales…"

After the forts north on the Bozeman Trail were closed in August 1867, Fort Fetterman was the sole U.S. Army presence near Powder River country, home to still-warring Sioux, Cheyenne, and Arapaho. Although the Oregon Trail was fifteen years past its peak of traffic, those who did use it valued the safety Fort Fetterman offered.

The fort was enlarged and, by the mid-1870s, was one of the best equipped in the West. Its story is one of the people who passed through, rather than of the actions its garrison

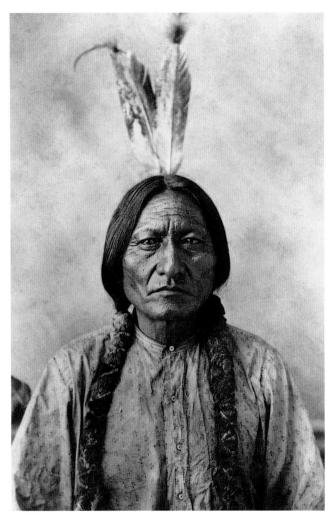

Holy man and war leader Sitting Bull believed throughout his life (ca. 1831-1890) that any contact with whites would weaken traditional Teton Sioux culture. MONTANA HISTORICAL SOCIETY

saw. Jim Bridger was here in 1868, supervising the wagon trains that carried furnishings and equipment away from the Bozeman Trail forts for use at other posts. Martha Jane Canary—Calamity Jane—supposedly passed through during her teamster days, or possibly when she followed miners of the Black Hills gold rush. James Butler "Wild Bill" Hickok may have played a hand or two of poker here on his own path around the West.

But mostly, Fort Fetterman served as the staging place for the last large army expeditions against Plains Indians, in the latter 1870s. From here, General George Crook led three marches into Sioux and Cheyenne country. The Civil War veteran was an experienced Indian fighter, having gone up against the Paiutes in eastern Oregon and the Apaches in Arizona. In the opinion of William T. Sherman, then general of the army, Crook was the army's greatest Indian fighter of all time. (One of Crook's techniques, adopted by other officers, was using Indian scouts.) The Indian leader Crazy Horse, himself a brilliant strategist, is said to have stated that Crook was the army officer to be feared the most.

Right: From here, General Crook led the column that Sioux and Cheyenne prevented from reaching the Battle of the Little Bighorn. FRED PFLUGHOFT

Below: No, the army didn't use disposable plates.
FRED PFLUGHOFT

In 1901, photographer L.A. Huffman joined a party visiting the Battle of the Rosebud, site of General George Crook's defeat by Sioux and Cheyenne. MONTANA HISTORICAL SOCIETY

In June of 1876, though, Crook met his match—in warriors led by Crazy Horse, Sitting Bull, and Crow King of the Sioux, and the Cheyennes Dull Knife, Two Moons, and Little Wolf. Pulling out of Fort Fetterman, Crook led a column of 1,000 infantry and cavalry troops north through Powder River country to Montana. With them were 250 Crow and Shoshone warriors, and 206 Crow and Shoshone aides. Supply wagons and spare horses and mules added to the cavalcade. Naturally, the dust cloud it raised was visible for miles.

To Crook, it seemed the combined Sioux and Cheyenne warriors came out of nowhere on June 17, near a canyon on Rosebud Creek in Montana. Crazy Horse led the opening charge. And more and more warriors appeared while the battle raged from 8:30 in the morning until noon. Finally, Crook retreated back into Wyoming. The victors were still relishing their win at a large encampment on the Little Bighorn the next week, when Lieutenant Colonel George Custer—having ignored warnings from his own Crow scouts—attacked it.

Custer's troops were one arm of a three-part pincer movement meant to surround hos-

Fort Fetterman's ordnance warehouse restoration. FRED PFLUGHOFT

winter food supply. Within a short time, the northern Plains Indian tribes all had surrendered or, like Sitting Bull's band, crossed the "medicine line" into Canada.

During the years that Fort Fetterman was garrisoned, something of a town grew up near it, grandly named Fetterman City. In 1882, the U.S. Army closed Fort Fetterman and moved on. Fetterman City lasted only four more years, until the town of Douglas was founded and stole its thunder. Buildings from both Fort Fetterman and its "city" were auctioned off, some becoming homes in Douglas or structures on area ranches.

A sheep rancher moved into the officers quarters and remodeled it as his home. The ammunition magazine became his chicken coop, and additions turned the ordnance building into his barn. In 1967, the Wyoming

tile Sioux and Cheyenne in southeastern Montana. Crook's defeated column had been another arm, the one that never made it to the Battle of the Little Bighorn.

After these two major defeats, the army attacked the Sioux and Cheyenne constantly throughout the winter of 1876-1877. Crazy Horse surrendered his own band in September 1877, because his people were worn down by continual battle, and hadn't had time and safety to hunt and preserve their

Department of Recreation purchased the Fort Fetterman site and these surviving buildings. The following year, the barn and house were restored to their original appearances.

Today Fort Fetterman is a Wyoming State Historic Site, open throughout the summer. Signs along the interpretive trail among building foundations tell their stories. In the ordnance building and in the officers' quarters, dioramas, artifacts, photographs, and other materials cover the Indians who once lived here, the rigors of life at Fort Fetterman, and the people who hoped to raise a city nearby. The second weekend in June brings back military life at Fort Fetterman, with living history performers, guided tours, Indian dancers, and more. In July, a similar weekend honors Fetterman City.

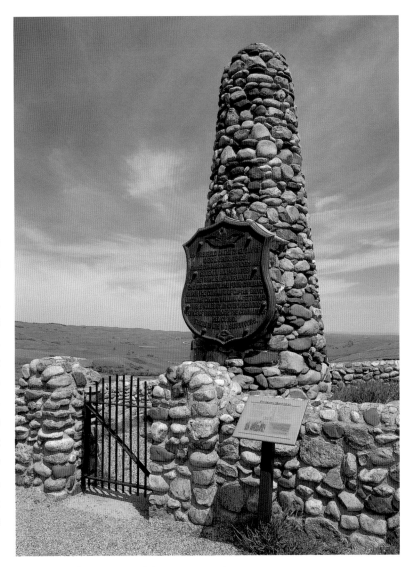

Memorial marker at the site of the Fettterman Fight. FRED PFLUGHOFT

Left: One of Fort Fred Steele's original buildings that survives. FRED PFLUGHOFT

Below: Fort Fred Steele, the Union Pacific Railroad, and an interesting visitor. WYOMING STATE ARCHIVES

～ FORT FRED STEELE ～

EST. 1868

ort Fred Steele, named for a Union general in the Civil War's Battle for Vicksburg, was built for and by the iron horse. It opened in June 1868, as crews were feverishly building the Union Pacific Railroad westward from Omaha toward it. Here they pushed the railroad across the North Platte River by bridge, a vulnerable spot. After Fort Steele's soldiers protected the railway builders, they stayed on to protect the bridge on the United States' first transcontinental line.

The Union Pacific was a railroad built by strong men with simple equipment, horses and mules. Tie-hackers cut the wood for cross-ties (2,500 were needed for each mile of track), and floated it down from the mountains for others to place on the surveyed path. The rail crew lived in train cars that crept behind them on rails they had laid that day.

In 1866, an eastern newspaper reporter captured the mind-numbing close drill that made it possible to put down a mile or two of track in one round of daylight. After the ties were laid:

"On they came. A light car, drawn by a single horse, gallops up to the front with its load of rails. Two men seize the end of a rail and start forward, the rest of the gang taking hold by twos, until it is clear of the car. They come forward at a run. At the word of command the rail is dropped in its place, right side up with care, while the same process goes on at the other side of the car. Less than thirty seconds to a rail, and so four rails go down to the minute. The moment the car is empty it is tipped over on the side of the track to let the next loaded car pass it, and then it is tipped back again, and it is a sight to see it go flying back for another load, propelled by a horse at

Union Pacific track layers pause just long enough for the slow camera lens, as they rush to lay at least two miles of track for the day. UNION PACIFIC HISTORICAL COLLECTION

Francisco. Twenty-one million times are those sledges to be swung…"

If ties and rails were ready and plentiful, a crew could complete three miles of track in a day. The record was eight and a half miles! These men worked every day of the week, for at least twelve hours. When they received a rare day off, their amusements were rough ones: gambling, drinking, and the fistfighting that seemed to accompany both. In eastern Wyoming, a newspaper coined the phrase "hell on wheels" to describe the often-violent railroad camps.

Along with the crowded dormitory cars, a construction train carried its own arsenal, and posted guards every moment. Plains Indians killed railroad surveyors, attacked building crews, and drove off stock in order to stop the progress of this permanent thing

full gallop at the end of sixty or eighty feet of rope. Close behind the first gang come the gaugers, spikers and bolters, and a lively time they make of it. It is a grand 'Anvil Chorus' that those sturdy sledges are playing across the plains. It is in triple time, three strokes to the spike…ten spikes to a rail, four hundred rails to a mile, eighteen hundred miles to San

On May 9, 1869, the eastbound Central Pacific train draws near the westbound Union Pacific train for the golden spike ceremony at Promontory Summit, Utah, marking completion of the United States' first transcontinental railroad.
UNION PACIFIC HISTORICAL COLLECTION

Set off at a distance for protection in case of explosion, the fort's powder magazine is its sole surviving intact structure. Built in 1881 of local stone, it replaced an earlier dugout. Fort Fred Steele wasn't heavily armed, and this would have housed signal flares and explosives for construction, along with ammunition. FRED PLUGHOFT

River and curved west through Medicine Bow to Fort Fred Steele, where it arrived on July 21, 1868—just a month after the fort was founded. The original track curved around the southwestern edge of the fort site.

The railroad continued westward through Green River and Evanston, entering Utah the following January. It met the eastward-building crews of the Central Pacific Railroad at Promontory Summit, Utah, on May 9, 1869—and for the first time people, freight, and precious mail could travel from the Atlantic to the Pacific across the United States by train.

Erecting Fort Fred Steele was quite an effort for its first garrison. The 300 men lived in tents, and could earn extra pay by volunteering to work on the permanent buildings. Guided by standard army blueprints, they used stone and pine from the immediate area. Civilians provided important skills, including blacksmithing, saddle-making, lumber milling, and wagon-wheel making. A civilian contracted with the army as sutler, or post trader; he obtained fresh food for the mess and

across the land. The army responded to the Union Pacific's plea for military protection, and one of the results was Fort Fred Steele.

The Union Pacific entered Wyoming in the southeast near Pine Bluffs in the fall of 1867, built over Sherman Summit, and reached Fort Laramie on June 7, 1868. From there the railroad went north through Rock

The Union Pacific proceeds through Fish Cut, in Wyoming, 1867. UNION PACIFIC HISTORICAL COLLECTION

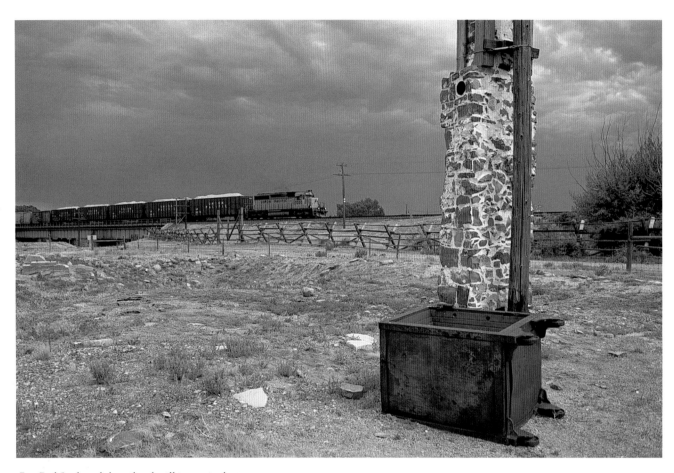

Fort Fred Steele and the railroad, still intertwined. FRED PFLUGHOFT

ran the post store that was open to the men and their families.

During the 1880s, Plains Indian warfare faded into the past, and in August 1886 the last garrison left Fort Fred Steele.

Across the tracks, a town had been platted, also becoming known as Fort Steele. Its residents served the railroad that created the town, receiving logs floated down the North Platte, and trimming them and soaking them in creosote (for preservation) to make railroad ties. Fort Steele also turned out fence posts.

Sheep ranching became important in this part of Wyoming once the railroad was there to carry its products to market, and a large shearing plant arose in Fort Steele. From it, the Union Pacific Railroad carried baled wool east to factories that would spin and weave it.

Sleepy little Fort Steele received an economic shot in the arm in 1915-1916, when it found itself right on another transcontinental first: the first coast-to-coast U.S. highway, known as the Lincoln Highway. It was built across Wyoming paralleling the Union Pacific Railroad (and future route of Interstate 80),

and bringing a new kind of traveler: the automobile tourist.

Funded by private as well as public money, the Lincoln Highway was to demonstrate that concrete roads were the thing of the future. It ran from Times Square in New York to Lincoln Park in San Francisco, and wasn't finished nationally until 1922. It benefited the town of Fort Steele throughout the years between the end of World War I and the onset of the Great Depression.

After crossing the North Platte from the north, the Lincoln Highway took pioneering "autoists" right through Fort Fred Steele, passing the remains of barracks then turning west across the parade ground.

In 1939, that situation ended when the highway was rerouted and the railroad-tie business ended. Today Fort Frederick Steele is a Wyoming State Historic Site, with interpretive signs among the remaining foundations and sole surviving building, the arsenal. It's a place to pause and wonder, to think about all the transportation changes this western land has witnessed.

In Wyoming in 1868, Union Pacific Railroad and military officials meet. From left: UP chief engineer Grenville M. Dodge, UP director Sidney Dillon, Gen. Phillip Sheridan, Mrs. J.H. Potter, Gen. John Gibbon, Mrs. John Gibbon, their son, General (and presidential candidate) Ulysses S. Grant, Gen. Frederick I. Dent, Katherine Gibbon, Mrs. John H. Frantz, Lt. William S. Starring, Francis Gibbon, Gen. William T. Sherman, Mrs. Potter's nurse, Alice Stemmer, Gen. W.S. Harney, UP financier Thomas Durant, unknown, Lt. John S. Bishop, Col. L. Cass Hunt, Gen. Adam Kautz, Gen. Joseph H. Potter. UNION PACIFIC HISTORICAL COLLECTION

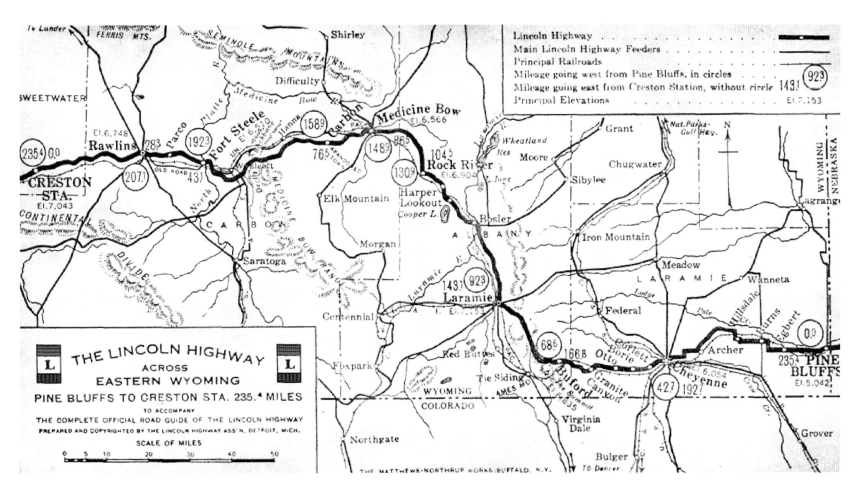

THE LINCOLN HIGHWAY
ACROSS
EASTERN WYOMING
PINE BLUFFS TO CRESTON STA. 235.⁴ MILES

TO ACCOMPANY
THE COMPLETE OFFICIAL ROAD GUIDE OF THE LINCOLN HIGHWAY
PREPARED AND COPYRIGHTED BY THE LINCOLN HIGHWAY ASS'N, DETROIT, MICH.

SCALE OF MILES
0 5 10   20   30   40   50

The first coast-to-coast named highway, the Lincoln Highway took very adventurous 1910s "autoists" across Wyoming, including through the grounds of old Fort Fred Steele. Not until 1922 did the road connect all the way from New York City to San Francisco.

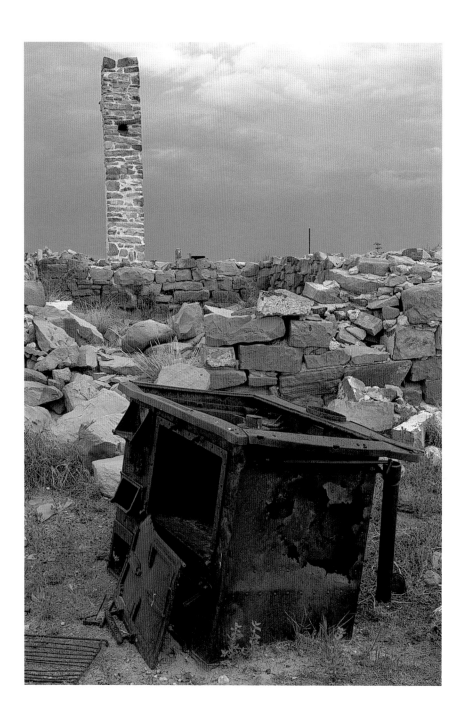

This stabilized chimney is one of Fort Fred Steele's meager remains.
FRED PLUGHOFT

Fort D.A. Russell

est. 1867

*H*ere's a riddle: Which historic Wyoming fort is both easy and impossible to find, except for once a year?

The answer doesn't involve magic, but is a short course in U.S. military history.

Fort D.A. Russell, a cavalry post, was established in the summer of 1867, and named for a Civil War hero killed in the Battle of Chantilly. It was a few miles from the Union Pacific Railroad's regional headquarters at Crow Creek Crossing, the place that became the city of Cheyenne. Protecting railroad builders was the garrison's first assignment. During the first winter, the men under command of Col. John D. Stevenson moved from tents into frame housing.

In 1884, after the railroad was finished and the Indian wars ended, the U.S. War Department looked at Fort Russell's location and decided to make it a permanent post. It sat about halfway between Canada and Mexico, and close to halfway between Los Angeles and New York. Now, eight infantry companies were assigned here, and more than two dozen brick buildings went up to house and serve them.

Soon those soldiers included three of the army's four regiments of black soldiers, the 9th and 10th Cavalry and the 24th Infantry. Indians are said to have nicknamed these men the "buffalo soldiers" because of their courage and endurance in battle.

By the time of the Spanish-American War in 1898, Fort Russell was the United States' largest cavalry post. From here, troops left to fight in both Cuba and the Philippines.

Fort Russell saw more changes in the years before World War I, first being enlarged to brigade size and tripling in physical size, and then becoming an artillery base. During the Mexican Revolution, 1913-1916, troops from Fort Russell were among those sent to protect the U.S.-Mexico border. Cavalry troops continued to serve at the fort, by now one of the nation's largest, until 1927.

Fort D.A. Russell "disappeared" in 1930, when President Herbert Hoover renamed it to honor

Francis E. Warren, Wyoming's first state governor and one of its U.S. Senators for nearly four decades. He also was father-in-law to General of the Armies John J. Pershing, who had served here commanding black troops early in his career. Warren, who died in 1929, had moved to Wyoming after serving in the Civil War (and winning the Congressional Medal of Honor). He built his personal fortune as a sheep rancher and landowner. Warren's successful political philosophy was that you "don't hunt ducks with a brass band."

Fort Francis E. Warren was an army post for nineteen years, further growing in size during World War II. In 1947, the United States Air Force was separated from the army, where it had existed for two decades. Two years later, the fort became Francis E. Warren Air Force Base. From 1958 until 1992, it was part of the Strategic Air Command, and it also was the first U.S. base exclusively handling intercontinental ballistic missiles.

Today, Warren Air Force Base is home to the 90th Space Wing, which commands Minuteman III and Peacekeeper missiles, and also to the 20th Air Force, which commands ICBMs. On the base's grounds is the modest red-brick building that was Fort D.A. Russell headquarters in 1900; today it houses exhibits and artifacts that tell the stories of Fort Russell, Fort Warren, and Warren AFB.

But come by during Cheyenne Frontier Days, the third week of July, and for three days Fort D.A. Russell is alive once again. Mountain men, 19th century troopers and their ladies are all here in the forms of living-history interpreters. The food, sights, sounds, activities, and goods for sale are as they were when the fort was a growing frontier cavalry post.

Today called "Frontier Manor," this piece of Fort Russell stands proudly at Warren Air Force Base.
FRED PFLUGHOFT

A surviving Fort D.A. Russell building now houses a frontier army museum at F.E. Warren Air Force Base.
FRED PFLUGHOFT

ᑫ INDEX ᑭ